O'AHU
Beach Access

O'AHU
Beach Access

A Guide to O'ahu's Beaches
through the Public Rights of Way

Katherine **Garner**
&
Carol **Kettner**

Mutual Publishing

Special thanks to **Mark Kettner** and **Carol Bonham** for their unwavering support and tenacious optimism.

Library of Congress Control Number: 2012935372

ISBN-10: 1-56647-975-4
ISBN-13: 978-1-56647-975-2

Cover design by Jane Gillespie
Interior design by Courtney Young

First Printing, May 2012
Second Printing, April 2013

Mutual Publishing, LLC
1215 Center Street, Suite 210
Honolulu, Hawai'i 96816
Ph: 808-732-1709 / Fax: 808-734-4094
email: info@mutualpublishing.com
www.mutualpublishing.com

Printed in Korea

Table of Contents

Map of Oʻahu

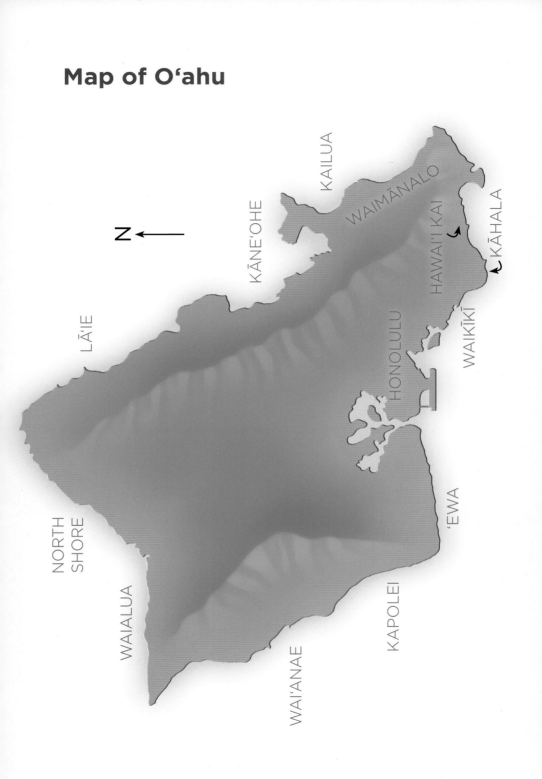

KAILUA

KĀNEʻOHE

WAIMĀNALO

HAWAIʻI KAI

KĀHALA

N

LĀʻIE

HONOLULU

WAIKĪKĪ

NORTH SHORE

ʻEWA

WAIALUA

KAPOLEI

WAIʻANAE

Introduction

id you know that Hawai'i's Supreme Court has repeatedly upheld your right to go to the beach? A city and county guideline states "where reasonable in urbanized areas there should be access every quarter mile." Hawai'i's unique political and cultural history as an independent nation has allowed the existence of public rights of way to some of the world's most beautiful hideaways. This book contains pictures, detailed descriptions and directions to the eighty-nine public rights of way (PROW) on the island of O'ahu. We've included bus routes, nearby parks and restroom facilities. We've described interesting facts and the history unique to each venue. We've outlined possible activities, marine life seen, and parking situations. So have an adventure and exercise your right to the public right of way.

Nestled in neighborhoods young and old, ritzy and downtrodden, are precious gateways to some of the earth's most spectacular vistas. We discovered our

first one bicycling through Kāhala on a bright June morning. We were intrigued by the bright blue sign, and chained our bikes to a pole and went exploring. This particular access was an easy climb down to a small triangle of sandy beach. We scrambled eastward over rocks and a concrete wall to find ourselves on the outskirts of Shangri La, the estate of the late tobacco heiress Doris Duke.

A light bulb went on. How about exploring all the public accesses on the entire island? We kept a written record of our adventure, took many pictures, and this book is the result.

We cross checked the eighty-nine accesses listed by the city and county with a property tax map and then reassigned our own numbering system. We begin in Waikīkī with access 1 and move consecutively eastward and counterclockwise

around Oʻahu's perimeter ending in Honolulu. At some accesses the friendly blue signs are missing. In one Kāneʻohe neighborhood, a man told us that two of his neighbors, "in collusion" had taken down the sign. Perhaps the publication of this book will bring about investigations and openings of those public rights of way, which have mysteriously disappeared over time.

The case of *Barba vs. Okuna* in 1980 was held at the Hawaiʻi Third Circuit Court where it was found that "the right to access is a necessary adjunct to the right to use and enjoy public trust areas and alienation of shoreline access was a breach of public trust."

In 1982, in the case of *Akau vs. Olohana*, The Hawaiʻi Supreme Court ruled: "The ability to get to a recreational area is as vital for enjoying it as having it in its natural condition." In recent years Oʻahu's Surfrider Foundation has played an active role in beach access litigation. Beach Access Hawaiʻi, a coalition formed by the Surfriders, organized an island-wide demonstration in February of 2008 to demand more beach access. Surfrider activists are on the lookout for beach right of way obstructions and support a 2009 bill that creates more leeway to challenge access blockers. We support their actions, and this book is our attempt to aide in any public access breach.

Table of Beach Parks and Accesses

	PARK OR PROW	BEACH	SWIM	SURF	BOAT	FISH	SNORKEL	KIDS	FACILITIES	BIKE	
1	Duke Kahanamoku BP	X	X	X		X	X	X	X		
	Fort DeRussy BP	X	X	X	X			X	X		
2	Gray's Beach	X	X	X			X	X	X		
	Royal Moana Beach	X	X	X	X			X	X		
	Kūhiō BP	X	X	X		X	X	X	X		
	Kapiʻolani Park	X	X	X		X	X	X	X		
	Queen's BP	X	X	X		X	X	X	X		
	Sans Souci BP	X	X	X	X	X	X	X	X		
	Lēʻahi BP		X			X		X		X	WAĪKIKĪ – KĀHALA
	Mākālei BP		X	X		X	X	X		X	
	Kuilei Cliffs BP		X	X		X	X	X		X	
	Diamond Head BP							X		X	
3	Kaʻalāwai Beach	X	X	X		X	X	X		X	
4	Kaikoʻo Pl.		X			X				X	
5	Kāhala Ave./ʻElepaio St.	X				X		X		X	
6	Kāhala Ave./Kālā Pl.	X				X		X		X	
7	Kāhala Ave./Hunakai Pl.	X	X			X	X	X		X	
8	Kāhala Ave.	X				X		X		X	
9	Kāhala Ave.	X				X		X		X	
10	Kāhala Ave.	X				X		X		X	
	Waiʻalae BP	X				X	X	X	X	X	
	Wailupe BP			X		X			X	X	HAWAIʻI KAI
	Kawaikuʻi BP	X		X		X			X	X	
11	Kalanianaʻole Hwy./ W. Halemaʻumaʻu St.	X		X		X				X	
	Kuliouʻou BP	X		X		X		X	X	X	
12	Paikō Dr.	X		X		X		X		X	
	Maunalua Bay BP			X	X	X		X	X	X	
13	Kōkeʻe BP			X		X				X	

	PARK OR PROW	BEACH	SWIM	SURF	BOAT	FISH	SNORKEL	KIDS	FACILITIES	BIKE	
14	Hanapēpē Lp./Moloa'a St.									X	HAWAII KAI
15	Koko Kai BP		X	X		X	X			X	HAWAII KAI
16	Lumaha'i St.					X				X	HAWAII KAI
	Hanauma Bay BP and Nature Preserve	X	X				X	X	X	X	HAWAII KAI
	Hālona Blowhole		X				X				HAWAII KAI
	Sandy BP	X	X	X		X			X	X	HAWAII KAI
	Makapu'u BP	X	X	X		X	X	X	X	X	WAIMANALO
	Kaupō BP	X	X			X		X	X		WAIMANALO
	Kaiona BP	X	X	X		X	X	X	X		WAIMANALO
	Waimānalo BP	X	X	X		X		X	X	X	WAIMANALO
17	Laumilo St./Wailea St.	X	X	X	X	X		X		X	WAIMANALO
18	Laumilo St./Pu'uone St.	X	X	X	X	X		X		X	WAIMANALO
19	Laumilo St./'Ala'ihi St.	X	X	X	X	X		X		X	WAIMANALO
20	Laumilo St./Mānana St.	X	X	X	X	X		X		X	WAIMANALO
21	Laumilo St./Hilu St.	X	X	X	X	X		X		X	WAIMANALO
22	Laumilo St./Ka'ulu St.	X	X	X	X	X		X		X	WAIMANALO
23	Laumilo St./Hīnālea St.	X	X	X	X	X		X		X	WAIMANALO
24	Laumilo St./Hīhīmanu St.	X	X	X	X	X		X		X	WAIMANALO
25	Laumilo St./'Ehukai St.	X	X	X	X	X		X		X	WAIMANALO
	Waimānalo Bay BP	X	X	X	X	X		X	X	X	WAIMANALO
	Bellows Field BP	X	X	X	X	X	X	X	X	X	WAIMANALO
26	Mokulua Dr./Lanipō Dr.	X	X	X	X	X	X	X		X	KAILUA
27	Mokulua Dr.	X	X	X	X	X	X	X		X	KAILUA
28	Mokulua Dr./Kaiolena Dr.	X	X	X	X	X	X	X		X	KAILUA
	Kailua BP	X	X	X	X	X	X	X	X	X	KAILUA
29	S. Kalāheo St./Ku'uniu St.	X	X	X	X	X		X		X	KAILUA
	Kalama BP	X	X	X	X	X		X	X	X	KAILUA
30	Dune Circle	X	X	X	X	X		X		X	KAILUA
31	Puealoha Pl./N. Kalāheo Ave.	X	X	X	X	X		X		X	KAILUA
32	N. Kalāheo Ave./'Ainoni St.	X	X	X	X	X		X		X	KAILUA

PARK OR PROW	BEACH	SWIM	SURF	BOAT	FISH	SNORKEL	KIDS	FACILITIES	BIKE
33 N. Kalāheo Ave./Kailuana Pl.	X	X	X	X	X		X		X
34 Kaimalino St./Launa Aloha Pl.				X	X	X			X
35 Milokai Pl.					X				X
36 Kāneʻohe Bay Dr.									
37 Kāneʻohe Bay Dr.				X					
38 *Not found*									
Kāneʻohe BP				X	X	X			
39 Ipuka St.				X	X				
Heʻeia State Park				X	X	X	X		
Laenani Neighborhood BP				X	X	X			
Kahaluʻu Regional Park				X	X				X
Waiāhole BP					X				X
Kualoa BP	X	X			X	X	X	X	X
Kalaeōʻio BP		X	X		X	X			X
Kaʻaʻawa BP	X	X			X	X	X		X
Swanzy BP					X	X	X		X
Ahupuaʻa ʻO Kahana State Park	X	X	X	X	X		X	X	X
Punaluʻu BP	X	X				X	X	X	X
40 Kaluanui Beach	X	X			X	X	X		X
41 Kaluanui	X	X			X	X	X		X
42 Kaluanui	X	X			X	X	X		X
Mākao Beach	X				X	X	X		X
43 Hauʻula Beach Remnant	X	X			X	X			X
ʻAukai BP					X				X
Hauʻula BP	X	X	X		X	X	X	X	X
Kokololio BP	X	X	X		X	X	X	X	X
Bath Tub Beach	X	X				X	X		X
Pounder's BP	X	X	X		X	X			X
Lāʻie BP	X	X	X		X	X			X
44 Kamehameha Hwy.	X	X	X	X	X	X			X

PARK OR PROW	BEACH	SWIM	SURF	BOAT	FISH	SNORKEL	KIDS	FACILITIES	BIKE
Lā'ie Point State Wayside					X	X			X
Mālaekahana State Rec. Area	X	X	X	X	X	X	X	X	X
Moku'auia Beach	X	X	X	X	X	X	X		
Turtle Bay/Kawela Bay	X	X	X	X	X	X		X	
Kawela Bay	X	X	X	X	X	X	X		
Waiale'e BP	X	X	X		X	X			X
Waiale'e Beach Right of Way	X	X	X		X		X		X
45 O'opuola St. and Sunset Point	X	X	X	X	X	X	X		X
46 Kahauola St.	X	X	X	X	X	X	X		X
47 Huelo St.	X	X	X	X	X	X	X		X
Sunset BP and Support Park	X	X	X	X	X	X	X	X	X
48 Kē Nui Rd.	X	X	X		X	X	X		X
49 Kē Nui Rd.	X	X	X	X	X	X	X		X
50 Kē Nui Rd.	X	X	X		X	X	X		X
51 Kē Nui Rd.	X		X						X
52 Kē Nui Rd.	X	X	X		X		X		X
'Ehukai BP	X	X	X		X		X	X	X
53 Kē Nui Rd.	X	X	X		X	X	X		X
54 Kamehameha Hwy.	X		X		X		X		X
55 Banzai Rock Beach Support Park	X	X	X		X	X	X		X
56 Ka Waena Rd.	X	X	X		X		X		X
57 Kē Iki Rd.	X	X	X		X	X	X		X
58 Kē Iki Rd.	X	X	X		X		X		X
59 Kē Iki Rd.	X					X			X
Pūpūkea BP and Uppers Surfing Support Park	X	X	X			X	X	X	X
Waimea Bay BP	X	X	X	X	X	X	X	X	
Leftovers Beach Access Park	X	X	X		X	X	X		
Kawailoa BP	X		X		X				
Chun's Reef Beach Support Park	X	X	X		X	X	X		
Laniākea Beach	X	X	X		X	X	X		

LĀ'IE

NORTH SHORE

PARK OR PROW	BEACH	SWIM	SURF	BOAT	FISH	SNORKEL	KIDS	FACILITIES	BIKE	
60 Pāpaʻiloa Rd.	X	X		X	X	X	X			NORTH SHORE
Haleʻiwa BP	X	X	X	X	X	X	X	X		NORTH SHORE
Haleʻiwa Aliʻi BP	X	X	X	X	X	X	X	X		NORTH SHORE
Kaiaka State Recreation Area		X	X		X		X	X	X	
61 Waialua Beach Rd.	X	X		X	X		X		X	
Puʻuiki BP	X	X	X		X	X	X		X	
62 Aʻu St. A	X		X		X		X		X	WAIALUA
ʻĀweoweo BP	X	X	X		X	X	X	X	X	WAIALUA
63 Aʻu St. B	X	X			X		X		X	WAIALUA
64 Crozier Brow	X	X		X	X	X	X		X	WAIALUA
65 Crozier Brow	X	X		X	X	X	X		X	WAIALUA
66 Makaleha BP	X	X	X	X	X	X	X		X	WAIALUA
67 Hoʻomana Beach									X	WAIALUA
Mokulēʻia BP	X	X	X	X	X	X	X	X	X	WAIALUA
Kaʻena Point State Park	X	X			X		X		X	
Keaʻau BP	X	X	X		X	X	X	X		
68 North Makau St.					X		X			
69 South Makau St.					X		X			
Mākaha BP	X	X	X	X	X	X	X	X		
70 ʻUpena St.	X	X	X	X	X		X			
71 Moua St.	X	X	X	X	X	X	X			WAIʻANAE
Mauna Lahilahi BP	X	X	X		X		X	X		WAIʻANAE
Pōkaʻī Bay BP	X	X	X	X	X	X	X	X		WAIʻANAE
Lualualei BP	X		X		X		X	X		WAIʻANAE
Māʻili BP	X	X	X	X	X		X	X		WAIʻANAE
Ulehawa BP	X	X	X	X	X		X	X		WAIʻANAE
Nānāikapono BP	X				X		X	X		WAIʻANAE
Nānākuli BP	X	X	X	X	X		X	X		WAIʻANAE
Tracks BP	X	X	X	X	X	X	X	X		WAIʻANAE
Kahe Point BP	X		X	X	X	X	X	X		WAIʻANAE

PARK OR PROW	BEACH	SWIM	SURF	BOAT	FISH	SNORKEL	KIDS	FACILITIES	BIKE	Region
72 Paradise Cove	X	X			X	X	X		X	KAPOLEI
73 Ko ʻOlina	X	X			X	X	X	X	X	KAPOLEI
74 Malakole Camp	X	X			X	X	X		X	KAPOLEI
Barber's Point BP	X				X		X		X	KAPOLEI
Nimitz Beach	X	X	X		X		X	X	X	KAPOLEI
White Plains BP	X	X	X				X	X	X	KAPOLEI
Oneʻula BP	X	X	X		X		X	X	X	KAPOLEI
75 Pōhakupuna Pl./Pūpū St.					X				X	
76 Oneʻula Pl.	X		X		X	X	X		X	
77 Parish Dr.	X				X	X	X		X	
78 ʻEwa Beach Rd.	X				X		X		X	
79 Fort Weaver Rd.									X	
80 ʻEwa Beach Rd.	X	X		X	X	X	X		X	ʻEWA
81 Fort Weaver Rd.									X	ʻEWA
82 ʻEwa Beach Rd.	X				X		X		X	ʻEWA
83 Fort Weaver Rd.									X	ʻEWA
84 ʻEwa Beach Rd.	X	X	X	X	X		X		X	ʻEWA
85 Fort Weaver Rd.									X	ʻEWA
86 ʻEwa Beach Rd.	X	X	X	X	X		X		X	ʻEWA
87 Fort Weaver Rd.									X	ʻEWA
88 ʻEwa Beach Rd.	X				X		X		X	ʻEWA
89 ʻEwa Beach Rd.	X			X	X		X		X	ʻEWA
ʻEwa BP	X	X	X	X	X		X	X	X	ʻEWA
Iroquois Point BP	X	X		X	X		X	X	X	ʻEWA
Keʻehi Lagoon BP	X	X	X	X	X			X		HONOLULU
Sand Island State Recreation Area	X	X	X		X		X	X		HONOLULU
Kakaʻako Waterfront Park		X	X		X		X	X	X	HONOLULU
Kewalo Basin Park		X	X	X	X		X	X		HONOLULU
Ala Moana BP	X	X	X	X	X		X	X	X	HONOLULU

Need to Know Before You Go

Before adventuring to the accesses and beach parks it is recommended you take a few minutes to familiarize yourself with Hawai'i's unique environment and potential perils. As in all outdoor activities, take time to arrive prepared so that you can have an enjoyable experience. Water, sunglasses, sunscreen, and appropriate footwear are essential. When exploring tide pools and reefs, rubber slippers quickly get chewed up and don't provide enough traction to keep you from slipping and falling. Don't forget your camera to capture memories of these hidden beach escapes.

The Environment

Just tiny dots on the world map, the Hawaiian archipelago is spread along 3300 kilometers of the northern edge of the Tropic of Cancer in the Pacific Ocean. This collection of atolls, reefs and islands extend from the Big Island of Hawai'i on the east to tiny Kure Atoll near the International Date Line on the west. Only eight of the easternmost islands are populated and they are considered "Hawai'i." Underwater volcanoes located on the Pacific Plate formed the islands. The plate is moving over an immobile hot spot that results in the arc of the Hawaiian Islands. The Big Island of Hawai'i, with active volcanoes, is the youngest of the island chain. O'ahu's dormant volcanoes are evidence of its fiery past. Landmarks such as Diamond Head, Koko Head, Punchbowl and parts of the Windward Side have seen the effects of erosion. Water and wind have dug away at the volcanic domes, leaving verdant valleys and spectacular sea cliffs behind to enchant visitors.

Weather

Hawai'i's balmy climate is one of its greatest attractions. Puffy white clouds dot the sky as they bring liquid sunshine in the form of showers and rainbows to the landscape. Mild temperatures and sunny days with occasional showers make almost every day one to explore the outdoors. Temperatures hover between 70 to 80 degrees on an average day, but expect more showers and wind in the winter when temperatures can drop into the low 60s on occasion. The normal weather pattern brings cooling trade winds from the northeast to counteract the moderate humidity. The east or Windward Side of the island tends to be the rainier side because the clouds hit the peaks of the Ko'olau Mountains and dump the rain on the verdant cliffs below. The Leeward Side west of the Wai'anae Mountains is hotter and drier.

There are only two seasons in Hawai'i, summer and winter. Summer months, May to September, bring fewer storms, so it is drier and hotter. Most of the time the cooling trade winds keep you comfortable, but it does get hot on the beach. Start in the early morning or late afternoon exploring the accesses and beaches. Try to avoid the midday sun, as it can be brutally hot on the sand and rocks. If you are out midday make sure you have plenty of water and sunscreen. Surf is up on the South Shore during the summer months, but with the shallow reef fronting most of the shore, waves tend to be in the one- to five-foot range. North Shore waters are flat and calm making beach entry more family friendly.

Winter months, October to April, bring more showers and wind with cooler temperatures. From time to time, Kona winds roll in from the south, which brings muggy "voggy" conditions. In recent years, the volcano has been producing volcanic ash, which is carried in the wind to Maui and O'ahu. Voggy days can make it hard to breathe and see. The air stings your eyes, and can do a number on your sinuses, but it brings spectacular sunsets with a burst of reds, oranges and pinks touching the clouds. Storms from the north often bring the world famous big surf that hit heights of twenty-five to thirty feet on the north and west shores. Many of the accesses on the North Shore change dramatically due to the high surf, but the South Shore is flat in the winter.

Ocean Safety And Lifeguard Services

There are twenty lifeguarded beaches in the county park system. Some of the parks listed are undeveloped parcels that have been randomly purchased by the city and county for future park expansion. Some of the county parks allow permit camping. Refer to the links below for more information.

Many of the accesses and beach parks listed here are not guarded beaches. Please take the following precautions before entering the water.

- Never go in the ocean alone.

- Use caution when entering and leaving the water; never turn your back to the waves.

- Stop and observe ocean conditions for at least ten minutes before entering the water.

- Beware of shoreline hazards; if the rocks are wet that means the waves could knock you off your feet. Stay back from sea cliffs and large breaking waves.

- Don't go out farther than you can swim.

- Beware and heed any posted warning signs.

- Beware of others around you, including boats, swimmers, snorkelers, surfers and ocean life!

- Don't leave valuables in your car.

- Wear sunscreen, no matter what the weather condition. Hats and loose-fitting clothes are suggested if you stay out in the midday sun.

- Drink plenty of water especially on hot muggy days to avoid heat exhaustion.

Beware of the following ocean conditions:

- **SHORE-BREAKS**—These can be dangerous depending on how large and hard the waves are. They form where the ocean floor changes from deep to shallow abruptly. If it is only a couple feet of water it is relatively safe to swim, but at places like Sandy Beach the shore-break is large and dangerous. Surfers and body boarders have suffered broken bones, neck injuries, and dislocated shoulders due to the force of the waves slamming down on them.

- **RIP CURRENTS**—Rip currents are also a danger for novice swimmers. These rapid flowing currents of water generally start near shore and move quickly out to sea. If caught in a rip current one should swim with the current until it fades out or swim parallel to shore. Do not try and swim against the current, as it will exhaust even the most expert swimmer.

- **ROGUE WAVES**—As stated above never turn your back to the ocean. Incoming waves usually come in sets and not all waves are the same height or force. They usually occur when there are high tides, high surf or stormy weather. Some of the accesses are along rocky coral shelves so be aware of your surroundings.

- **UNDERTOW**—Undertows are found near steeply sloped beaches in high waves. The backwash from the large waves flows out quickly and gets caught under the incoming wave. A swimmer can get tossed beneath the surface of the water, so it is better to swim out beyond the wave and wait for the set to take a break before trying to swim in.

Ocean Pests

Hawai'i's ocean is spectacularly clear and free from seaweed but there are some pests to beware of. Box jellyfish, Portuguese man o' war, eels, spiny urchins and the occasional shark are the most common creatures causing problems.

BOX JELLYFISH are regular visitors to the south and west shores arriving about ten days after the full moon. They hang around for three to four days and then disappear until the next full moon. They are clear and nearly transparent so you won't see them right away in the water. The body of the jellyfish is about one to three inches in size but the tentacles can reach up to two feet long. If you are stung, spray or pour liberal amounts of vinegar on the affected area. Take off the tentacles with a towel; don't use your fingers because you can be stung again. If you are at a lifeguarded beach, report the incident to the lifeguard. Stings can cause anaphylactic shock, so call 911 if victim should have hard time breathing or has muscle cramps, shortness of breath, or palpitations.

PORTUGUESE MAN O' WARS are frequent visitors to the windward shores. The body is a small clear bubble nearly undetectable in the water. They have long blue stinging tentacles that wrap around body parts. The sting is similar to a bee sting and is treated the same as the jellyfish stings.

STINGING LIMU can be a problem at some windward beaches during the summer months. The fine brown seaweed finds its way inside bathing suits producing a burning or itchy rash that can last anywhere from four to forty-eight hours. The burning may not occur immediately but washing with soap and water should help remove the filaments from the skin. Cool compresses or rubbing alcohol may help alleviate the pain. If there is persistent itching a one percent hydrocortisone cream applied to the area may bring relief.

SEA URCHINS are another hazard if walking on reefs. Be sure to clean as much of the spines of the urchin out of the wound as possible, as spines can survive for a long time inside the skin and add to discomfort and swelling. Soak the area in undiluted vinegar as long as possible as it will help dissolve the remaining parts of the urchin.

For more detailed information on treating wounds, bites, and stings, *All Stings Considered* by Craig Thomas M.D. and Susan Scott is an excellent resource book.

SHARKS—Considering Hawai'i is in the middle of a vast ocean full of a variety of shark species, the incidence of shark attacks is relatively rare. There are only a couple of shark attacks reported each year in the Hawaiian Islands. The most common shark to attack in Hawai'i is the tiger shark which ranges in size from six to eighteen feet with the average size about twelve feet long. Their blunt nose and vertical bars on the side easily identify these sharks. Tiger sharks come near shore most frequently between the fall and spring months especially after heavy rains when stream runoff produces new food sources that are swept out to sea. Since they have a keen sense of smell, tigers can smell blood from miles away and can locate prey even in murky waters. Tigers' diet consists of smaller fish, birds, turtles, other dead animals, and even garbage. Tigers are seen most frequently in the early morning and twilight hours, as this is their typical feeding time. Following a few safety guidelines can greatly minimize the risk of a shark attack.

Don't enter the water after heavy rains or when murky water is present. Avoid entering the water alone when engaging in ocean activities; always have a partner. Avoid wearing shiny or high contrast clothing as sharks can easily see contrast. Do not enter the water if you are bleeding or have open cuts. If spear fishing, drag fish a good distance behind you.

Endangered Species

THE HAWAIIAN MONK SEAL, listed on the critically endangered species list, is found only in tropical waters. These seals have been hunted to near extinction with only about 1,100 remaining. They are the last of the tropical monk seal species left on the planet. Most of the seals live in the Northwest Hawaiian Islands in the Papahānaumokuākea Marine National Monument. There are several hundred seals still in the main Hawaiian Islands. We spotted the seals on the South Shore near the Kapolei accesses, along the North Shore at Ka'ena Point and near Waialua. We were lucky enough to see a mother and baby near

Turtle Bay. If you see a monk seal on shore keep your distance. They are agitated by humans and become aggressive if they feel threatened. Hawaiian Monk Seals are protected under two different federal laws and fines for violations can be as high as $20,000.

GREEN SEA TURTLES, affectionately known as "honu," are frequent visitors to the beaches on Oʻahu despite their status on the endangered species list. They are the largest of hard-shelled turtle species and were valued by the early Hawaiians for their shells and meat. Over-harvesting, degradation of habitat, and Fibro papilloma, a disease that causes tumors on its body, have lead to the turtle's demise. Recent efforts to save the turtles include state laws, federal protection and international laws resulting in fines up to $100,000 for hunting, injuring, or harassing them. If you see them, enjoy them from a distance but please don't touch or bother them.

Aloha ʻĀina

"Aloha ʻĀina" means love the land and aloha ʻāina is a deep part of Hawaiian culture. When out enjoying the accesses and beach parks, please be a kind visitor and show your aloha spirit. Many of these accesses are in quiet neighborhoods; be careful not to disturb the homeowners. One homeowner near an access complained that people would leave trash on the beach and use her hose to shower off before leaving. Remember the beach is public domain up to the high water mark; you have every right to be there, but be considerate of the residents in the area. Pack your trash, there are cans at most accesses.

Transportation

RENTAL CARS are available at the airport and at many hotels and kiosks in Waikīkī. Although renting a car gives you the freedom to schedule your adventures on your own time, it is best not to travel during peak traffic times. The morning rush hour starts as early as 5:30 AM and doesn't clear until after 9:00 AM. Evening rush hour can start as early as 3:00 or 3:30 PM and doesn't clear up until 7:00 PM. Roads in and out of Waikīkī are poorly marked, and there is a plethora of one-way streets with maddening on and off ramps to the freeway that make little sense. Make sure you are equipped with good maps or a GPS in your car. We have done our best to give you specific instructions to the accesses and beach parks, but most streets have Hawaiian names that can be hard to read and locate. Never leave any valuables in your car—that's what hotel safes are for! Rental cars are easily identified for theft and you don't want to ruin your vacation by having to replace lost credit cards and other valuables.

THE BUS public transportation system on Oʻahu is an excellent alternative to driving the congested roadways. It is extensive and you can take the bus to most of the sites listed in this guide. Bus information has been given for each area of the island with bus numbers serving that route. For routes, schedules, and times call (808) 848-5555 between 5:30 AM to 10:00 PM HST or visit their website http://www.thebus.org/

BICYCLING is one of the more pleasant ways to explore the island. Bikes are allowed on buses, most of which are equipped with bike racks to accommodate two bikes. There is no additional charge for bringing your bike with you. The State Department of Transportation provides trail maps for novice to experienced cyclists at the website listed below. Be sure to wear appropriate safety gear, and heed all traffic signs for a safe and enjoyable ride. There are a couple of shops around the island that rent bikes; check in the yellow pages under 'bicycle renting' for current information. Kailua has an experimental bike rental program where you can rent bikes off racks at two different street locations. One station is located at 151 Hekili Street near the popular Boots and Kimo restaurant and the other station is located on Kailua Road just past Hahani Street Each station has seven beach cruiser type bikes available to rent for a nominal fee; the first half hour is free. Maps can be found at the Bike Oʻahu website http://Hawaii.gov/dot/highways/Bike/Oahu

Camping Information

STATE PARKS—There are eleven state parks listed in this guide, although camping is only allowed at three of them: Ahupuaʻa ʻO Kahana, Mālaekahana and Sand Island State Recreation Area. Camping permits are available on-line and can be requested up to one year in advance. There is a minimal fee per night with a limit of a five consecutive night stay, no camping is allowed on Wednesday and Thursday nights. Additional information is available at:

State Parks P.O. Box 621, Honolulu, HI 96809
Telephone: (808) 587-0300

http://www.hawaiistateparks.org/index.cfm
http://www.hawaiistateparks.org/camping/fees.cfm

CITY AND COUNTY PARKS—Camping is allowed at thirteen beach parks on Oʻahu. Permits are obtained from the main office located at 650 South King Street in the Frank Fasi Municipal Building at the Parks Permit section on the ground floor or at Kapolei Satellite City Hall or Wahiawā Satellite City Hall between the hours of 8:00 AM to 4:00 PM. The free permits are required. Camping is only allowed from 8:00 AM on Friday to 8:00 AM on Wednesdays. Permits are available only two Fridays before the desired dates. A word of caution: if you choose to camp on any holidays the chances of obtaining a permit are slim because people are known to line up days in advance to wait for the opportunity to apply for a permit. Check the website for availability and number of campsites. Some campgrounds are only open in the summer. http://www.co.honolulu.hi.us/parks/camping.htm

Hiking Trails

Although most of these accesses can be reached without using the trail system, this link has been included because there are a few beach hikes that are on established trails. Kaʻena Point on the northwestern tip of Oʻahu is one such trail. There are downloadable maps at the Na Ala Hele Trail and Access System website at http://hawaiitrails.ehawaii.gov/home.php

Ocean Safety

For more detailed ocean safety, beach sign guide and surf information refer to the following links.

http://www.co.honolulu.hi.us/esd/oceansafety/

http://oceansafety.soest.hawaii.edu/?i=oahu

BEACH SIGNS

http://www.co.honolulu.hi.us/esd/oceansafety/beachsigns.htm

SNORKELING INFORMATION

http://www.tropicalsnorkeling.com/oahu-snorkeling-hawaii.html

http://www.hawaiisnorkelingguide.com

http://www.hawaiisnorkelingguide.com/

SURF INFORMATION

http://www.thesurfingsite.com/Surf-Spots-Oahu.html

http://www.surf-oahu.com/

http://www.surfrider.org/stateofthebeach/05-sr/state.asp?zone=IS&state
=hi&cat=ba

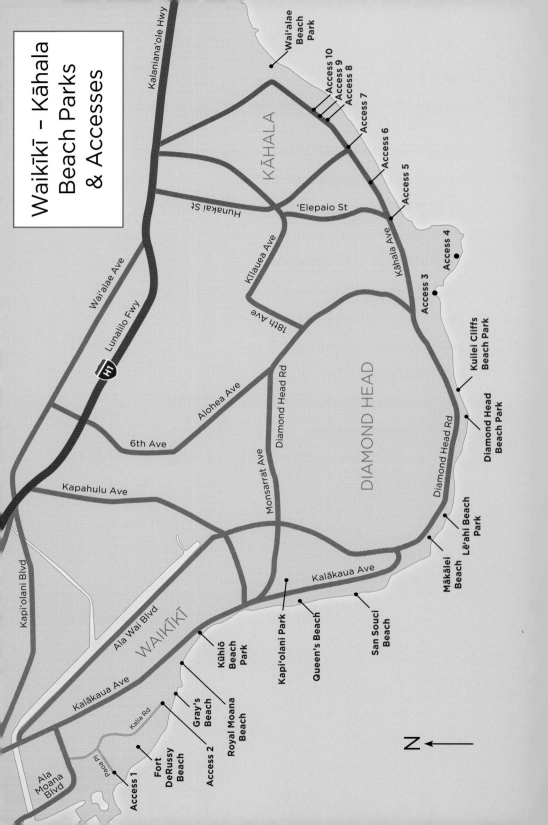

Waikīkī – Kāhala
Beach Parks
& Accesses

WAIKĪKĪ TO KĀHALA
Beach Parks and Accesses 1 to 10

With its skyscraper hotels and throngs of tourists, Waikīkī is one of the most sought after destinations in the world. Along with the sunburned tourists, nightlife sizzles with many bars open into the early morning hours. Located on the southern shore of Oʻahu, this heartbeat of Honolulu has long been a place of beauty and pleasure. A retreat for Hawaiian Royalty since the 1800s, Waikīkī was named "spouting waters" for the fresh water springs and streams that once fed its wetlands. The Ala Wai Canal was dug to drain these former wetlands. Located between the Ala Wai Canal and Diamond Head, Waikīkī's beaches have world-class waves for surfers. Native Hawaiians invented surfing centuries ago, but missionaries discouraged the sport. Some Hawaiians kept surfing at Waikīkī and it later became known to the world when local boy Duke Kahanamoku won three gold medals in the 1912 Stockholm Olympics. After the Olympics, Duke travelled the world demonstrating surfing. Waikīkī became known as the "birthplace of modern surfing" when tourists flocked to Duke's hometown, and the beaches that were his playground. While touring Waikīkī Beach, you will likely walk past a statue of Duke Kahanamoku and his surfboard. Created by sculptor Jan-Michelle Sawyer, the statue was dedicated on August 24, 1990. Duke's arms are open in greeting, and leis given by grateful fans drape his neck and sway in the trade winds. In 2011, Duke Kahanamoku Beach was chosen as #3 in the world by Dr. Beach on his annual list of the ten best beaches in the world. Dr. Stephen Leatherman has been publishing his famous annual list of America's Best Beaches since 1990. The area is easily explored by bicycle; the paths abound around Diamond Head and throughout Kāhala. This course is routinely used by all types of athletes and provides some of the best scenery on the island.

Public transportation on Oʻahu is via "The Bus," an excellent and reliable island-wide system. The number 8 bus shuttles between Waikīkī and the Ala Moana Shopping Center every ten minutes. Once at Ala Moana Shopping Center, one can transfer to other parts the island for only $2.50. Towns further east past Diamond Head Park can be reached by taking Routes 14, 22, and 23. The Waikīkī Trolley's green, red and pink lines go to 30 stops. The green line or scenic trolley arrives every 35 minutes and can take you as far east as access

5. The pink line serves as a shopping tour and shuttle. The red line is a historic tour of both Waikīkī and Honolulu. One day, four day and seven day passes and packages are available for purchase at http://waikikitrolley.com/.

Access 1
Duke Kahanamoku Beach Park
PAOA PLACE / WESTERN END OF WAIKĪKĪ BEACH

From Ala Moana Boulevard traveling east, turn right at Hobron Lane. Follow the road to the "T" and turn left. This public right of way (PROW) is .25 miles from Ala Wai Boat Harbor. There is no parking available on Paoa Place so it is best to access the free parking lot at the Ala Wai Boat Harbor. There is free and paid public parking allowed on the left facing the Hilton Lagoon and in the lot closest to the ocean. A paved walking path surrounding the Duke Kahanamoku or the Hilton Lagoon starts here and leads to the right of way. Walk west past the Hilton Hawaiian Village to the entrance to a park, which is the actual location of the right of way.

It is easy to see why this area is one of the top ten rated beaches in the world for 2011 by "Dr. Beach." There are picnic tables, barbecues, and a playground located under big shady trees looking out at the sandy beaches and the turquoise blue waters beyond. Lifeguards are on duty year round and there are restrooms and showers. With its wide white sandy beach and shallow water this is an excellent family beach spot with a bounty of water adventures to choose from. Swimming, windsurfing, snorkeling, surfing and stand up paddle boarding

are common activities here because of the calm waters. Beach equipment, food and drink concessions, and catamaran cruises are also available. The boat ramp located just to the right is the launching point for submarine tours. Surf sites beyond the reef are "In Betweens," "Kaisers," "Number Fours" and "Rock Piles."

Fort DeRussy Beach Park
KĀLIA ROAD / WESTERN END OF WAIKĪKĪ BEACH

From Ala Moana Boulevard travel east approximately one mile where it will merge with Kalākaua Avenue. Continue on Kalākaua Avenue, turn right on Saratoga Avenue where you will find street metered parking. Follow Saratoga Avenue until you reach the "T" where it turns into Kālia Road. The access is sandwiched between the Outrigger Reef Hotel and the Halekūlani Hotel. Keep going straight until you reach the park. This popular park has a shady grass grilling area, sand volleyball courts, and aquatic rentals. Amenities here include lifeguard, food and drink concessions, picnic tables, playground, showers, and toilets. A boardwalk fronting the Halekūlani leads east at the water's edge, where turtles can be seen frolicking in the waves. There are a number of restaurants where you can enjoy views of the palm-lined shores and turquoise waters while dining. Rental stands dot

the beach with surfboards, outrigger canoe rides, catamaran rides, beach chairs, and umbrellas available for rent. Lifeguards are on duty. Restroom facilities are located inside the hotel lobbies, or to the west at the edge of Fort DeRussy Park. Picnic tables and food and drink concessions are located in the park area. Swimming, windsurfing, surfing, snorkeling, stand up paddle boarding, and canoeing are some of the activities that can be enjoyed at this access. The surf site "Number Threes" is just off shore.

Access 2
Gray's Beach
KĀLIA ROAD / MIDDLE OF WAIKĪKĪ BEACH

Parking and main directions are the same as to Fort DeRussy Beach Park, but you will turn left at the "T" where it turns into Kālia Road. The access is a pathway between the Westparc and Halekūlani hotels. Gray's Beach abuts the Halekūlani Hotel. It is often crowded and is named for a small inn that stood here in the early 1900s. Fort DeRussy restrooms are close by. A lifeguard station in central Waikīkī is near the police station. Swimming, windsurfing, snorkeling, stand up paddle boarding, and canoeing are doable here.

Royal Moana Beach
MIDDLE OF WAIKĪKĪ BEACH

Royal Moana Beach is next along this 1.5-mile Waikīkī Beach strip. The access is off Kalākaua Avenue. Parking once again is available at Queen Kapiʻolani Park. Royal Moana Beach, located between the Royal Hawaiian Hotel and the Sheraton Moana Surfrider, is an extremely crowded beach. "Wakiki Beach Boys" are here to assist you with surfing, stand up paddle boarding, outrigger canoe rides and a host of other activities. Activities for beginners and the fainthearted abound here because of the calm waters. Beach equipment and food and drink concession stands populate the shoreline. Restrooms are in the hotels and at Fort DeRussy Park. This beach is also named for an inn from the early 1900s.

Kūhiō Beach Park
2453 KALĀKAUA AVENUE

This park is located between the Sheraton Moana Surfrider and the intersection of Kalākaua Avenue and Kapahulu Avenue. The Duke Kahanamoku statue, the Prince Kūhiō statue and the Stones of Kapaemahu (the wizard stones) are located here. The stones represent four beloved legendary healers who came to Hawai'i from Tahiti. Prince Kūhiō Park was the site of Prince Kūhiō's home. In 1918, Kūhiō removed the high fence around his home and opened the beach to the public. Four years later the property

was given to the city when he died of heart disease. It was officially dedicated as Kūhiō Beach Park in 1940. The park supports a stone pier, which juts out into the ocean. Walk to the end for a stunning vista of Waikīkī. Officially known as the Kapahulu Groin, the pier is an extension of a storm drain that runs under Kapahulu Avenue.

All these beaches are shallow with a sandy bottom, gentle waves, and good swimming. The water is protected by reef or wall, making the area safer for children and beginning swimmers. Lifeguards are on duty. The sky is the limit as far as available rentals: catamarans, outrigger canoes, kayaks, surf boards, stand up paddle boards, beach umbrellas, beach chaise lounges, beach chairs, air mats and tubes, boogie boards, masks, snorkel, and fins. Surfing lessons can be found here at any of the beach boy shacks. Restrooms, showers and picnic tables are plentiful. A branch police station is located at Royal Moana Beach. Waikīkī's famous surf sites, "The Paradise," "Number Threes," "Populars," "Queens," and "Canoes," are just off shore and offer many opportunities for neophytes to catch their first ride on a surfboard.

Kapiʻolani Park

The oldest and largest public park in Hawai'i, Kapi'olani Park was donated in 1877 by King David Kalākaua and named after his wife, Queen Kapi'olani. This public park is also home to the Honolulu Zoo and Waikīkī Shell. Huge banyan trees here along with a bandstand and benched seats shade the queen's statue. Consisting of three hundred

acres, there's plenty of space for picnicking, sports games, biking, and jogging. The park includes tennis courts, soccer fields, and an archery range. There is no beach access but free and metered parking stalls surround the park's perimeter and are just across the street from Waikīkī Beach's eastern end. This is a perfect place to start a biking adventure. Follow Kalākaua Avenue until you reach Diamond Head Road. Turn right and follow the bike path signs. The path extends over Diamond Head Road and splits into Diamond Head Road and Kāhala Avenue. Stay to the left, and follow the road around the base of Diamond Head. This road also leads to the entrance to the Diamond Head Crater Park. Turn right on 18th Avenue. Follow down the hill to Kīlauea Avenue. Turn right and continue through Kāhala to Makaīwa Street (across from Kāhala Mall). Turn right on Makaīwa Street, take the first right on Moho Street, then turn right on Kealaʻolu Avenue. This takes you to the far end of Kāhala. Proceed along Kealaʻolu Avenue to Kāhala Avenue. Waialua Beach Park and the Kāhala Resort are to the left and on the right is a scenic ride past the mansions of Kāhala with many accesses to stop and explore along the way.

Queen's Beach
2715 KALĀKAUA AVENUE / EAST END OF WAIKĪKĪ

Located between The Kapahulu Groin and the Waikīkī Aquarium, the beach is named for Queen Liliʻuokalani's house, which was located here. It is also known as "Gay Beach," because since the 1970s, gay men have been congregating here. There is much family entertainment as well, including "Sunset on the Beach." At 4 PM on Saturdays and Sundays music and entertainment begins and food booths are set up. Around sunset, movies are shown on a cinema-sized screen with the moonlit ocean as a backdrop. Volleyball nets are posted and games are constant. Near the entrance is a bronze sculpture called "Surfer on a Wave." The park contains restrooms, showers, barbeque grills and picnic tables. There's a small covered pavilion in a grassy area behind the beach where restrooms and a snack bar are located. The waves are gentle due to the reef, and swimming is a common activity. Lifeguards are on duty year round. "Cunha's" and "Publics" are two popular surf sites just off shore. The big wave surf site, Cunha's, is located straight out from the wall. "Walls," a surf break reserved only for body boarders, is located nearby and named for the Kapahulu Groin.

Sans Souci Beach Park
2863 KALĀKAUA AVENUE / EAST END OF WAIKĪKĪ BEACH

"Sans Souci" is French for "without a care." Like many others the beach is named after a hotel, which once operated here. Located between the War Natatorium and New Otani Kaimana Beach Hotel, this beach is also called "Dig

Me Beach" after the notorious bikinis and buff bodies seen here. On Kalākaua Boulevard just past the Waikīkī Aquarium, turn right into a curving driveway that ends with a parking lot directly in front of the Natatorium. The Natatorium was once an official Olympic-sized pool and active memorial, but is now a safety hazard that has been closed for years due to its crumbling ocean front pool. Lifeguards are on duty with restrooms and showers located at the east end of the Natatorium. Public phones are located in the grassy area near the hotel. There is a beach access ramp for handicapped here that will take them out to the water's edge. This one hundred-foot wide strand of white sand and coral is perfect for small children as it is protected by the reef from wave action. The area is great for swimming, snorkeling and diving a little farther out beyond the reef. Expert swimmers, triathletes in training and kayakers also frequent the beach to access the waters beyond the reef through "Kapua Channel," which also leads to "Tongs," "Old Mans," and "Canoes," three popular surf sites. There is a jetty and pier for the Elks Club and Outrigger Canoe Club members located at the east end of the beach. Writer Robert Louis Stevenson of *Treasure Island* fame lived here when he was in Hawaiʻi.

Mākālei Beach Park
3111 DIAMOND HEAD ROAD

This .7-acre pearl of a park used to be private property, but the city purchased it in 1972. It can be reached by following Kalākaua Avenue through Waikīkī until it intersects Diamond Head Road. Turn right on Diamond Head Road it is approximately .1 miles on your right. There is no parking or restrooms available here. The rock wall fronting the ocean makes this a popular wedding site, but inhibits swimming. A small pocket of sand on the western side of the seawall is just wide enough for sunbathing. The park has picnic tables, showers and some big shady trees. There is an elevated concrete walkway fronting the estates that connects to Lēʻahi Beach Park to the east. This dog-friendly beach is a popular access point to the following surf sites: "Rice Bowls," "Tongs," "The Winch," "Radicals," "Graveyards," "Suicides," and "Sleepy Hollows."

Lē'ahi Beach Park
3187 DIAMOND HEAD ROAD

This charming 1.3-acre oceanfront park is easily spotted behind a wrought iron fence. Once a beachfront home, the well-manicured lawn is dotted with coconut palm trees. The Dillingham family donated the land to the City and County of Honolulu in 1960. Access to the ocean is down a flight of lava rock stairs that leads to a coral-rock-strewn and sandy beach and a number of popular surf sites as well as swimming, snorkeling and fishing. Due to the limited access, the area is dog friendly without having to worry about disturbing beachgoers.

Diamond Head Beach Park
3300 DIAMOND HEAD ROAD

Located at the top of Diamond Head Road, this park includes two acres of sea cliffs with a narrow sandy beach that's ideal for tide pool excursions. Parking is on Diamond Head Road but don't leave any valuables in your car as break-ins occur here. Descend to the beach following the steep dirt path in front of the parking area. Surf breaks abound here for paddle boarders, windsurfers, body boarders and surfers. The surf breaks include "Kuilei Cliffs" or "Cliffs," at the eastern end of the park, "Lighthouse" which is directly in front of the lighthouse, and "Suicides," which is at the western end of the park. The reef is shallow so beware at low tide while paddling out. Waves are pretty consistent here but the winds affect how clean the conditions are. On calm days, in an absence of waves, there is snorkeling and tide pooling around the reefs. There are no facilities here except a hose in place of showers.

Kuilei Cliffs Beach Park
3451 DIAMOND HEAD ROAD

The park lies at the foot of Diamond Head, between the Diamond Head Lighthouse and the residential community of Kaʻalāwai. Containing three popular drive-in panoramas, the eleven-acre beach park features a narrow beach backed by sea cliffs.

Honolulu sculptress Kate Kelly created a memorial to Amelia Earhart (1898-1939) located on the second lookout. She was the first woman to fly across the Atlantic Ocean, and in 1935 she was the first person to fly alone from Hawaiʻi to North America. She was on her way to Hawaiʻi from New Guinea in 1939, but she never reached her stopover on Howland Island, and in fact was never seen again.

Access to the park is through a paved walkway on Diamond Head Road, located between two of the lookouts. There's a parking lot on Diamond Head Road just beyond the lighthouse. Swimming is not recommended because

of the shallow coral reef. However, surfers find a paradise here as the reef generates waves almost every day, and it is a lot less crowded here than in Waikīkī. When the trade winds are strong, this area is also a popular spot among windsurfers. Surfing, windsurfing, fishing and snorkeling are popular here. There are no lifeguards, but showers and parking are available. Surf sites include "Lighthouse," "Wailupes," and "Boneyards."

Access 3
Ka'alāwai Beach
KULAMANU PLACE

Though a little hard to find, this access provides some exquisite views of oceanfront homes as well as water activities. From the Diamond Head lookout proceed east on Diamond Head Road until you reach "Triangle Park," a tree-filled triangular grassy park. Stay in the right lane and veer to the right on Kulamanu Street, follow until you reach Kulamanu Place. There is no parking on Kulamanu Place so park on Kulamanu Street and walk down one block to the access. This beach is also known as "Cromwell's" or "Duke's." To the west is a pleasant walk with views of oceanfront estates. It is somewhat rocky and shallow so it isn't good for swimming. Two surf breaks are located off this access. One is Ka'alāwai Point, better known as "Brown's." It is a big wave spot but risky as sharks frequent the area. The other surf break is "Ka'alāwai Beach" which is a body-boarding break. There is some swimming and snorkeling near shore in the area fronting Shangri-La, the Doris Duke Estate. Doris Duke, heir to the Duke Tobacco and Duke Power fortunes, built her home here in 1937 and had the rocks dredged to create a private boat dock for her husband's yacht. The dock is no longer used so it provides entertainment for local children, who jump off the walls to the sandy ocean bottom complete with lava rock stairs to exit and try again. To get to the area fronting the estate you must navigate over low rock walls around the cove to the east of the access or wade through the shallow water. There are no public facilities of any kind.

Access 4
KAIKO'O PLACE

From Kāhala Avenue turn right on Pāpū Circle. Follow the road to the "T"; park on Pāpū Circle because no parking is allowed on Kaiko'o Place. Walk to the right down Kaiko'o Place. As the road levels the access is located on the left. The access sign has been removed, but the access is located directly behind the No Parking sign. Surfers are rewarded with million dollar views after hopping over the rocks to reach the "Black Point" surf break. Access to the ocean is to the left across the rocks or to the right in a shallow cove that is protected from the waves. It is relatively close to shore with sharp coral rocks, and not suggested for beginners. No public facilities. Surf sites off shore include "Cromwell's" or "Duke's" and "Kaiko'o's."

Access 5
KĀHALA AVENUE AT THE END OF 'ELEPAIO STREET

Continuing on Kāhala Avenue the next access is hidden behind overgrown palms. It is marked by a sign indicating a left turn on 'Elepaio Street to get to H1/72 Highway. Parking is available on Kāhala Avenue or on 'Elepaio Street. Old wooden fences and lush foliage line the dirt path that leads to steps go-

ing down to a rock-strewn beach. The beach is narrow with only some pockets of sand during low tide. There is a large storm drain located at the end of this access with a pipe leading out a few hundred yards to deeper waters. Surfers use this lane to reach the Black Point surf site located just beyond the point. Rock seawalls hiding luxurious homes line the mauka (mountain) side of the beach. To the right about one hundred feet down is a small cove before the land stretches out to Black Point. To the left is a small pocket of sand good for wading at high tide. Fishing in the shallow waters is another activity that is suitable here. No public facilities.

Access 6
KĀHALA AVENUE AT THE END OF KĀLĀ PLACE

Twin lion statues mark the driveway to the left of this access. Parking is along Kāhala Avenue or across the street on Kālā Place. The sandy path situated between stone walls and a chain-link fence leads to a narrow sandy patch, which is swallowed by the ocean at high tide. Rock walls line the coast with pockets of sand fronting them. There is a channel that leads to the outer reef where large waves break.

Access 7

Nicknamed "Mother's" Beach because of the sandy pockets that make swimming safe for small keiki (children), this is one of the more popular accesses in the area. Although one local family had staked out the end of the access as their picnic spot, there was still ample room on the narrow strip of beach. At high tide there is about ten feet of beach. Directly in front of the access is a pipeline that leads to the outer reef. Fishermen were observed at the edge to the outer reef some one hundred yards out. It is a lovely stroll along the beach starting at this access and heading north about .5 miles to the Kāhala Hotel and Resort. There are lots of places to laze the day away listening to the waves lapping on the shore. The water is just deep enough in some spots to cool off but it is too shallow for swimming and snorkeling. This is an especially romantic spot for moonlit walks when the full moon rises over Koko Head. The shimmering water and palm trees swaying in the breeze will fulfill your fantasies of life in paradise.

Access 8

This access and the next one are located on either side of a large oceanfront estate with a stucco and wood fence. Although this access looks like a private driveway that ends in a green-slated chain-link fence from the road, the access is open to foot traffic. Parking is allowed on Kāhala Avenue. The construction fence on the right and debris strewn in front of the lot on beach side don't make

this the most pleasant of the Kāhala beach accesses. Although once out on the beach there is a nice ten- to twenty-foot strip of sand to sunbathe on. There appears to be a channel that leads through the shallow inner reef to a couple hundred feet off shore where the waves are breaking. Fishing along the outer reef is a popular activity as the water is only about ankle deep before the drop-off.

Access 9
KĀHALA AVENUE AT THE END OF KŌLOA STREET

Located on the north side of some oceanfront estate property, this access is a little more inviting. Again, there is no parking on the private drive leading

to the beach, although there is ample parking on Kāhala Avenue. The views of Koko Head and the southeastern coastline are spectacular, especially if there is an early morning shower blowing through. The beach was mostly deserted on most days. With the tall coconut palms swaying in the wind and the extraordinary beachfront estates as the backdrop, this is easily one of the most scenic spots on the island. The white sand is hard-packed making for an easy walk down to the shoreline.

Access 10
KĀHALA AVENUE

This access is directly behind the bus stop and the 133A emergency access sign. It looks like forbidden territory but don't let the private property sign scare you. Although there is no parking allowed on the private driveway, pedestrians are allowed access through the wrought iron fence at the end of the driveway. Parking is allowed on Kāhala Avenue. There is a twenty-foot-wide beach strand here with coconut palms and naupaka bushes fringing the shoreline. There is some coral scattered around the shallow reef, so swimming is not recommended. It looks like a fishermen's narrow path leads to the outer reef.

Wai'alae Beach Park
4925 KĀHALA AVENUE

Wai'alae Beach Park is named for a freshwater spring nearby that used to serve Hawaiian royalty. This park is also known as Kāhala Beach Park and is located at the end of Kāhala Avenue just steps from the Kāhala Hotel and Resort. This park is one of the most popular wedding sites on the island. Grassy areas under coconut palms lead up to a white sand beach—a perfect spot for sunrise wed-

dings. There are vine-covered pavilions, restrooms, showers and plenty of picnic tables. A canal divides the park with a bridge crossing over to the other side. A short walk down the beach towards the hotel leads to a small peninsula that is a romantic landscaped walkway complete with palms and lush foliage. There is limited swimming in front of the hotel but swimming is not recommended at the park. Kayaking and fishing are the preferred activities here with an occasional windsurfer. Just out from the hotel about 150 yards is a surf break good for body boarding when the south side surf is up. Surf site "Razors" is on the west side of the channel.

Waikīkī History

When the first Polynesians arrived in Waikīkī sometime between 400 and 1200 AD, they discovered its rich wetland and over time established settlements, stretching from valley to reef along the coast. The land was extremely well suited for wetland farming, dry land crops, and fishing.

In 1450 AD, King Mailikukahi, ruler of O'ahu, moved his capital to Waikīkī. Under this gracious king, O'ahu's coastal management of fish, mussel, seaweed, and shellfish populations reached unprecedented heights. Added to this rich ocean bounty was an abundance of fresh water, major resource development of fishponds, wetland farms of taro and other crops. Waikīkī also became a primary place of healing and recreation for Hawaiians as the soothing vista and balmy waters brought calm and relaxation. Mailikukahi, beloved by his people, welcomed all to Waikīkī, and set high standards as a host.

Jewel that it was, sometime after 1760 Waikīkī caught the eye of the powerful King Kahekili of Maui. He waged war, conquered O'ahu and sent his son Kalanikūpule to rule from Waikīkī. In the late 1700s, Kamehameha the Great invaded Waikīkī and defeated King Kalanikūpule in the famous battle of Nu'uanu Pali. After this battle Kamehameha established all the islands under his rule and united them into one kingdom. Newly discovered by Europe, the United States, and Japan, Hawai'i suddenly had a new market for its economy. Honolulu Harbor became a place of import for trade and commerce. Kamehameha decided his new capital needed a major port of call for merchant ships, and moved the capital from Waikīkī to Honolulu with her harbor.

In spite of the move of the capital to Honolulu, Waikīkī continued its popularity as a place of healing. As the family of Kamehameha grew, Waikīkī became a Royal Retreat for his dynasty to relax and play. In the late 1800s, King Kalākaua gained fame bringing esteemed guests to his private beach house. Robert Louis Stevenson of *Treasure Island* fame was one of those guests.

In 1828, the Hawaiian population was devastated by the introduction of western diseases such as measles. With no immunity, in a very short time the population of native Hawaiians dropped from approximately 450,000 to less than 30,000. The result was a catastrophic loss of workforce and cultural practitioners. Waikīkī agricultural production was sharply curtailed, the wetlands were abandoned, and Waikīkī declined as a food production center. Hawaiian royalty continued to play in Waikīkī and when King Kalākaua created Queen Kapiʻolani Park in 1877, Waikīkī's playground popularity grew. This three-hundred-acre park designed in the style of New York Central Park once featured a horseracing track complete with grandstand. It was destroyed in 1914 partly due to public outcry against gambling.

In the 1880s, bathhouses began popping up in Waikīkī. Precursors to the first hotels, they offered rooms for overnight stays. The Moana was Waikīkī's first resort, opening in 1901. In 1927, Waikīkī tourism escalated for rich and famous mainlanders with the construction of the glamorous Royal Hawaiian hotel. This new star joined with the Moana Hotel to bring luxury to a world-renowned paradise.

Waikīkī became a larger haven after the draining of Waikīkī's swampland. The swamp was declared a health hazard by Board of Health director Lucius Pinkham, mostly due to mosquitoes. By 1928, the land was restructured into the Ala Wai Canal and 5,000 subdivided lots. For the next two decades Oʻahu continued as a vacation spot exclusive to the stars.

After the bombing of Pearl Harbor on December 7, 1941, Waikīkī was no longer filled with tourists. The U.S. Navy leased the Royal Hawaiian as a rest and relaxation center for military personnel. Although the Moana remained open as a guesthouse, it was always at full occupancy with defense-related servicemen. The beach was a maze of barbed wire during this time but sun, sand, and water were still enjoyed by persistent soldiers.

After World War II, newer larger commercial airplanes were developed. With easier and more economical travel, tourism boomed in Waikīkī, which now catered to a more middle class clientele. Over the next five decades, hotels, restaurants, and bars popped up everywhere.

In recent years, Waikīkī has been hard hit. Waikīkī, relying heavily on tourism, has seen island tourism statistics dip significantly as a result of global financial and other crises. Occupancy and revenue plummeted once again in 2010 and many big hotels as well as small businesses have gone into foreclosure and bankruptcy. Yet Waikīkī remains a dream destination for many. No doubt this playground in paradise will bounce back along with the rebounding economy.

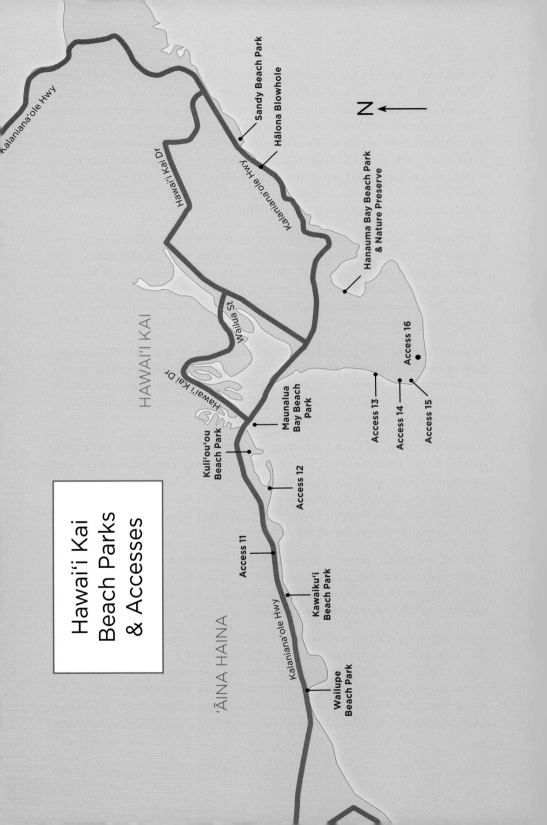

Hawai'i Kai
Beach Parks
& Accesses

HAWAI'I KAI

'ĀINA HAINA

Kalaniana'ole Hwy

Hawai'i Kai Dr

Hawai'i Kai Dr

Wailua St

Kalaniana'ole Hwy

Kalaniana'ole Hwy

N

Sandy Beach Park

Hālona Blowhole

Hanauma Bay Beach Park
& Nature Preserve

Access 16

Access 13

Access 14

Access 15

Maunalua
Bay Beach
Park

Kuli'ou'ou
Beach Park

Access 12

Access 11

Kawaiku'i
Beach Park

Wailupe
Beach Park

HAWAI'I KAI
Beach Parks and Accesses 11 to 16

Named for its founder Henry Kaiser, Hawai'i Kai is at the easternmost end of the sunny South Shore of O'ahu. The scenic drive hugs the coastline, displaying splendid homes nestled on slopes overlooking the ocean. Southern glimpses, of sapphire sea are visible through palm-tree lined parks. Two beach parks, Wailupe and Kawaiku'i, are along Kalaniana'ole Highway before reaching the first of the public accesses. Four beach parks abut various accesses. Kuli'ou'ou and Maunalua are the westernmost and they are superior beach parks. Maunalua Beach Park, much bigger with a boat harbor, supports small seagoing vessels. Kōke'e Beach Park and Koko Kai Beach Park have stunning views but no public amenities. World renowned for snorkeling, Hanauma Bay Beach Park and Nature Preserve is located further east on Kalaniana'ole Highway. After passing the entrance to Hanauma Bay keep heading east on Kalaniana'ole Highway and you will reach Sandy Beach Park. Visually the accesses become more breathtaking as you head east; at numbers 14, 15, and 16, ocean, earth, and man combine to become spectacular entertainment and a five star experience.

From Waikīkī take Ala Wai Boulevard to McCully Street, turn right, pass over the bridge and take the next right on Kapi'olani Boulevard. Stay in the left hand lane, turn left at the entrance to H1 east, and continue east on the freeway. It becomes route 72 or Kalaniana'ole Highway just past Diamond Head.

Bus Routes 1, 22, 23, or 58 reach accesses 11 and 12. For accesses 13 to 16 take Routes 1, 22, or 58.

Bike Routes

A dedicated bike lane along Kalaniana'ole Highway provides easy access to all the parks and PROWs in the area. There are two options for starting the bike adventure. For the shorter ride, start at Wailupe Beach Park and proceed east on Kalaniana'ole Highway. For the longer ride start in Kāhala at Wai'alae Beach Park, exit the park to the left and turn right on Keala'olu Avenue. Follow the bike lane to the intersection at Wai'alae Avenue, turn right and continue to the entrance to Kalaniana'ole Highway. Three beach parks and accesses 11 and 12 can be seen before the bike path ends in Hawai'i Kai at Lunalilo Home Road. To continue out to accesses 13 to 16 turn right at Lunalilo Home Road.

For the experienced rider who feels comfortable with climbing hills on narrow shoulders and steep heights you can continue along Kalaniana'ole Highway around the eastern tip of the island with frequent stops to enjoy the breathtaking cliff views. Just past Sandy Beach turn left at the light on Kealahou, turn left again at Hawai'i Kai Drive and climb over "heartbreak hill" to connect up with Lunalilo Home Road. Turn left and follow the road back to Kalaniana'ole Highway. Koko Marina Shopping Center is located at the corner with numerous options to stop for refreshments or a full meal before returning back to the start of your biking adventure.

Wailupe Beach Park
5045 KALANIANA'OLE HIGHWAY

The first beach park on Kalaniana'ole Highway is Wailupe Beach Park. Wailupe in Hawaiian means "kite water." It is believed that this area was a popular site for flying kites due to the steady trade winds. Surfing and fishing are preferred activities at this quiet neighborhood park. The Wailupe peninsula was a fishpond dredged around the perimeter and backfilled to create the housing subdivision. If one is willing to paddle out there are a couple of breaks for intermediate surfers beyond the reef. With break names such as "Secrets" and "Misery," going with a local who is familiar with the area would be the best approach to surfing here. There is a private boat harbor for the residents on the western side of the peninsula. There are no lifeguards on duty here, but there are parking, restrooms, showers, and picnic tables.

Kawaiku'i Beach Park
5475 KALANIANA'OLE HIGHWAY

Just across from the steep ridge of Hawai'i Loa is this quaint beach park, which is a popular wedding and picnicking site. Picnic tables are nestled under the shady trees and coconut palm trees on the grassy four-acre park. There is a fresh water spring located near the eastern edge of the park, giving the park its name, which means "united water." No water activities here except for fishing. Parking is available along with restrooms and showers.

Access 11
KALANIANA'OLE HIGHWAY AND WEST HALEMA'UMA'U STREET

This access is located five hundred feet past West Halema'uma'u Street on Kalaniana'ole Highway, next to a bus stop and directly before Niu Stream.

Continue past Niu Stream and park on Niuiki Circle to the east. There is no beach access on Niuiki Circle.

This fifteen-foot-wide dirt strip between two chain-link fences is easy to spot with the 128A sign at the entrance. Thirty feet of sand lead to a rocky reef covered by shallow waters. The reef extends about .5 miles from the shore. Westward toward Diamond Head is a neighborhood of attractive beachfront homes perfect to stroll in for a glimpse of island life at its best. Although it is too shallow to swim, kayaking, and surfing are popular. A surf site called "Seconds," is located beyond the reef, which provides surfing opportunities free of the crowds in Waikīkī. Palm trees provide shade for picnicking along this mostly deserted beach.

Access 12
PAIKŌ DRIVE

With parking available on the quiet cul-de-sac, this access is located next, about halfway down Paikō Drive on the right hand side next to the 127A sign. At high tide there is only about ten feet of beach. Walk east along the shoreline .2 miles to Paikō Lagoon Wildlife Estuary. Though not open to the public, one can view the lake and might be lucky to see a Hawaiian coot, stilt, or other endangered marsh bird. Walk westward to see elegant traditional kama'āina estates, their yards open to the ocean, and quaintly mixed with trendy, contemporary manors. In about a quarter mile, this tranquil, serene beach ends in a cove of houses with seawalls.

Kuliou'ou Beach Park
101 BAY STREET

To get to Kuliou'ou Beach Park turn right on Bay Street off Kalaniana'ole Highway just before the light on Kawaihae Road. Follow Bay Street until it dead-ends at the park. Kuliou'ou means "sounding knee." The ancient Hawaiians used a small drum tied to the knee while performing the hula; it's likely the park's name refers to the sounding of the knee drum. Kuliou'ou Park's narrow sand beach and flat shallow reef allows access to several surf sites located outside the reef called "Tunas," "Manantan's," and "Turtles." Parking, picnic tables, restrooms, and showers are available. Ocean activities include fishing, surfing, and kayaking.

Maunalua Bay Beach Park
6499 KALANIANA'OLE HIGHWAY

Maunalua means "two mountains." The name refers to two very prominent peaks at the east end of the bay, Koko Head and Koko Crater. Henry J. Kaiser developed Maunalua Bay Beach Park in the late 1950s. He dredged coral and other material from Maunalua Bay and pumped it into low places on the shore to create the park as well as a boat channel and ramp that are parallel to the eastern end of the park. In January 1960, Kaiser donated the new park to the City and County of Honolulu. Maunalua Bay Beach Park is well used by boaters, outrigger canoe paddlers, kayakers, fishermen, and picnickers. The Hui Nalu Canoe Club, one of the oldest outrigger canoe clubs in Hawai'i, keeps its fleet at the west end of the park where the canoe hale or hall is located. Public amenities include parking, picnic tables, restrooms, and showers.

From Lunalilo Home Road proceed makai to the first left at Poʻipū Drive. Turn left, then turn right at Nāwiliwili Street. Located at the end of Kōkeʻe Place, where street parking is available, the access is through a vacant lot and down a steep and slippery path to a rock ledge beach. Bathroom facilities are at Maunalua Bay Beach Park about two miles away. Someone has nailed boards into a tree making a makeshift bench which overlooks the ocean, but it has fallen into disrepair and is no longer safe to sit on. The beach here is made up of a rocky ledge, so no swimming or snorkeling, but a good place for fishing and tide pooling at low tide. Kōkeʻe means "to bend" and was named after a place on Kauaʻi that borders Waimea Canyon. This is a popular entry to "Pillars" surf site. To the west is a small beach and boat harbor where Henry Kaiser who, as mentioned, once had his estate. The boat harbor is a great fishing spot and on an average day is lined with people and their fishing poles. Henry Kaiser, who largely developed Hawaiʻi Kai, built his oceanfront home here on seven acres in the 1960s. He wanted a private boat dock to come right up to his house, so he dredged through the coral reef off shore to build the entrance to the harbor. The home has an interesting history, being bought and sold numerous times. Previous owners, besides the eccentric Mr. Kaiser, included brothers Alfred and Monte Goldman, who were heirs to a fortune left them by their father, the inventor of the shopping cart. Japanese billionaire Gensiro Kawamoto paid

$42.5 million for the buildings on the land in 1988. He later gave the property up in a dispute with landowner Kamehameha Schools over the $1 million a year lease for the land. The property was put up for auction in 1997. When it failed to sell, they broke the property up into three fee simple lots. Fred and Annie Chan, high-tech business owners who graduated from University of Hawai'i, bought two of the parcels. The last parcel sold was in 2005 for a whopping $15.9 million to a Merrill Lynch executive and his movie star wife. The main building stands as an empty shadow of its former grandiose self.

Access 14
HANAPĒPĒ LOOP JUST PAST MOLOA'A STREET

Unfortunately this scenic access was recently closed due to hazardous conditions; probably the stairway and collapsing tree branches have made it unsafe. The city erected a chain-link fence across the opening to restrict access. Recent communications between the residents and city regarding restoration of the stairs have resulted in the city refusing to make improvements at this time or take down the chain-link fence. Street parking is available for this access. The entrance can still be seen filtered around gnarled trunks and leaves, the sunlight illuminates graffiti on concrete walls and a rusted handrail creating an eerie ambience. The stairs lead to a rocky and coral strewn beach, which was only ten feet wide at high tide. This must have been a popular access to "China Walls" surf site, as we saw at least a half dozen surfers and boogie boarders when we visited. They climbed a rocky embankment to our east and disappeared until we saw them riding waves westward below us, narrowly missing the jutting rock walls around the beach. Chances are these daring young men have been coming here since boyhood. Luckily this area can still be accessed for ocean sports via the Koko Kai Beach Park.

Access 15
Koko Kai Beach Park
END OF HANAPĒPĒ PLACE

Parking for this access is available on Hanapēpē Loop. Although it is listed as a park there are no facilities here. Access is through the vacant lot and down a steep path. The signs here read "warning—drownings have occurred here." This is also an entry point to "China Walls," "Walls," and "Fingers" surf sites. You will notice a narrow rock sticking straight up out of the ocean. It is called "the Finger" and surfers use this rock to jump into the water and access "Fingers." The waves smash onto the seawalls and as one local told us: "Only expe-

rienced surfers do 'Chinas,' other people might get munched." After the surfer, we saw sea turtles, fisherman, and cliff divers. The hypnotic crash of waves against towering rock walls is a dramatic backdrop for watching daring surfers up close and personal.

Access 16
END OF LUMAHA'I STREET

From Lunalilo Home Road take the first left at Po'ipū Drive, continue past Nāwiliwili Street and veer right. Turn left on Lumaha'i Street, veer right and continue to the end of the street. The access is located on the right next to a moss rock wall. The 119A access sign marks the path. Enter the access through a long, sharp sloping path surrounded by ironwood and rubber trees. The two minutes downhill is only slightly

strenuous, but be prepared to huff and puff your way back up. A possible aviary is on the west side of the path, as we heard many different birds chirping. We navigated the steep incline then took a few seconds to catch our breath and absorb all the activity around us. We watched in horror as three daredevils took turns jumping off the ledge into the churning surf sixty-five feet below. The rocks shook as waves coursed through an underwater spitting cave located under our feet. This perilous diving site is aptly named "Spitting Caves." At least a dozen fishermen with tents were fly-fishing from a western point above us; sixty feet below them a metal ladder is located at the water's edge to reach the ledge above. This is a great whale-watching spot in the winter.

In her June 18, 2006 article "Increase of Drownings Spurs Push to Educate" *Honolulu Advertiser* reporter Suzanne Roig warns of the danger at this site. "Despite warning signs and occasional patrols by lifeguards on personal watercraft when conditions become particularly dangerous, drownings and rescues are a regular occurrence at two popular cliff-diving places: Spitting Caves and China Walls."

Hanauma Bay Beach Park and Nature Preserve
7455 KALANIANA'OLE HIGHWAY

Hanauma Bay Nature Preserve is south on Hanauma Bay Road from Kalaniania'ole Highway. One of the most popular snorkeling spots in the world, Hanauma Bay was also popular with Ancient Hawaiian royalty or "ali'i." Fishing was abundant and the currents gentle. A shallow reef fringes the narrow beach at the head of the bay keeping the near shore waters calm year round. Hanauma means either "hand wrestling" or "curved bay." Hand wrestling was popular among the ali'i and legend tells of a beautiful Hanauma chieftain's daughter whose two suitors hand-wrestled for her hand in marriage. The beach park became a marine life conservation district (MLCD) in 1967. State law prohibited MLCD fishing, increasing marine life populations and providing a unique visual experience to snorkelers, scuba divers, and swimmers. *Conde Nast* magazine named Hanauma Bay Nature Preserve as the best U.S. beach in 2004.

Hanauma Bay has an education center, both equipment and food concessions, shuttle service, and gift shop as well as parking, picnic tables, restrooms, and showers. The stream of visitors to this park is constant. If you want to be sure of a parking spot, we suggest an early start.

Hālona Blowhole
KALANIAN'OLE HIGHWAY

Just one mile east of Hanauma Bay is a lookout and parking area for this popular natural attraction. The ocean puts on a spectacular show with sprays of water being shot up as much as thirty feet in the air as the waves force ocean water through an underground lava tube. Best viewing conditions are on windy days at high tide when the ocean is churned up. On clear days the islands of Moloka'i, Maui and Lāna'i can be spotted in the distance. Whales frolic off the coast in winter months and at the nearby Hālona Cove giant sea turtles can often be spotted swimming in the protected cove. Swimming, snorkeling, and scuba diving are popular activities here when the ocean is calm.

Only experienced divers should go out here and care should be taken due to strong currents flowing out to sea, lack of easy exits, lots of sharp rocks, and no lifeguards nearby.

Sandy Beach Park
8801 KALANIANA'OLE HIGHWAY

The only sand beach along a rocky coastline, this beach is aptly named. Sandy Beach is world renowned for its body boarding and bodysurfing sites and its high proportion of ambulance calls. The steep, hard crashing waves generate rip currents. Visitors new to the beach often misjudge the waves and get into trouble.

"Tourists see little ten and twelve-year-old kids that have been doing this for some years and think they can do it, too," said lifeguard Billy Gordon in 2002.

"Attention on the beach: For those who are unfamiliar with this beach, it has the highest rate of broken backs and necks in the nation. This is not a beach for children or weak swimmers. There are safer beaches ten minutes up the road. If you need information, come up and talk to us," is a common megaphone message when the beach is crowded.

There are plenty of warning signs and lifeguards have been stationed daily at Sandy's since February 1971.

"Pipe Littles" and "Half Point" are two bodysurfing sites in front of the comfort station. "Full Point" is a surf site at the east end of the beach. Shore casting is another popular activity here at the northern end of the park area across from Kealahou Street. Parking, picnic tables, showers, and restrooms are available to the public.

Hawaiʻi Kai History

Early Hawaiians used the 532-acre Kuapā (which means fishpond) Lagoon as a fishpond and reinforced the natural sand bar with stone walls. The pond stewards placed removable sluice gates in the stone wall which allowed ocean and bay water to enter the pond through the gates during high tide. During low tide the current would reverse toward the ocean. Fishponds like this were an important part of ancient Hawaiian agriculture. Each Hawaiian island or "mokupuni" was divided into several wedge-shaped "moku" running from the mountain crest to shore. Oʻahu was divided into six moku. Each moku was divided into ahupuaʻa, narrower wedge shaped land sections that likewise ran from mountain to sea. Each ahupuaʻa was ruled by an aliʻi or local chief and administered by a "konohiki" or steward.

Kuapā Pond was part of an ahupuaʻa that was eventually vested to Bernice Puahi Bishop and on her death became part of Bishop Estate. She was the great-granddaughter of King Kamehameha I and the last descendant of his royal line. Her private estate is one of the largest in Hawaiʻi. The revenues from Bishop Estate are used to operate Kamehameha Schools, established in 1887 according to Pauahi's last will and testament.

Kaiser leased a six thousand acre area including Kuapā Pond from Bishop Estate to create Hawaiʻi Kai, a marina community of fourteen thousand homes. He planned to build Queen's Beach resort, but plans were dropped after much community protest. Nearly all the low-lying lands surrounding the marina have since been developed, and neighborhoods now extend back into valleys and up the separating ridges.

The western and most scenic of the Hawaiʻi Kai public rights of way are located in a posh neighborhood called Portlock. The area is named after Captain Nathaniel Portlock who was captain of two British vessels for King George and Queen Charlotte sailing from the Big Island. He came ashore in this area in search of fresh water. The community lives on the western tip of Koko Head peninsula with Hanauma Bay located on the eastern side. The homes in this neighborhood routinely fetch prices in the multimillion-dollar range.

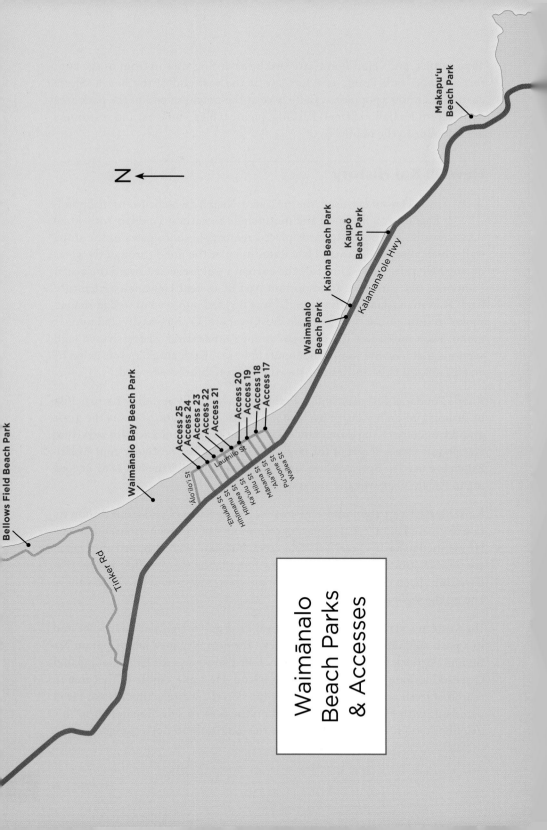

N ←

Makapuʻu
Beach Park

Kaiona Beach Park

Kaupō
Beach Park

Kalanianaʻole Hwy

Waimānalo
Beach Park

Access 25
Access 24
Access 23
Access 22
Access 21
Access 20
Access 19
Access 18
Access 17

Laumilo St

Āloʻiloʻi St

Ehukai St
Hihimanu St
Hīnalea St
Kaʻulu St
Hilu St
Mahana St
ʻAlaʻihi St
Puʻuone St
Wailea St

Waimānalo Bay Beach Park

Bellows Field Beach Park

Tinker Rd

Waimānalo
Beach Parks
& Accesses

WAIMĀNALO
Beach Parks and Accesses 23 to 26

The panoramic view of the windward coast from the Makapuʻu lookout is one of the most breathtaking vistas on the island. With the powder white sand beaches, and the shallow turquoise water meeting the azure skies spotted with white puffy clouds, one could spend the entire day taking in the view. The name Makapuʻu, which means "bulging eyes," comes from a legend about a rock located at the mouth of a cave directly below the cliffs. A supernatural woman named Makapuʻu manifested herself in the rock and bumps on the rock resemble her eyes thus the name "bulging eyes." Two islands can be seen off shore to the east. The closest one is "Mānana" or "Rabbit" Island, the farther island is "Kāohikaipu" or "The One that Gathers Island," most likely due to the flotsam clustering there. Rabbit Island gets its name for two reasons; one is that the island looks like a rabbit's head with its ears back. The other reason is because up until 1994 rabbits inhabited the island. They have since been eradicated because they became a threat to the native birds nesting on the island. Both islands are bird sanctuaries and require permission from the Board of Land and Natural Resources to land there. Kāohikaipu is also known as Black Rock or Kākalaioa Rock. There is good scuba diving off the coast between to two islands with many tropical fish but caution should be taken due to strong currents and sharks. White tipped and reef sharks are commonly found in this area because they are attracted to the fish.

To reach the area, take Ala Wai Boulevard to McCully Street, turn right at Kapiʻolani Boulevard and stay in the left lane. Take the entrance to H1 freeway east. The freeway ends and turns into Kalanianaʻole Highway until it reaches the easternmost end of the island where it turns towards the north. The beach rights of way are located in between Waimānalo Beach Park and Waimānalo Bay Beach Park also known as Sherwood Forest. Take the first right after Waimānalo Beach Park on Wailea Street to Laumilo Street. This is the beginning of this three-quarter-mile stretch of beach accesses 23 to 26.

If traveling by The Bus take route 57, 77 (Shuttle), or the 89 Express Bus. Bus stops are on Kalanianaʻole Highway with a short walk to Laumilo Street.

A bike path begins along Kalanianaʻole Highway at Makapuʻu Beach and extends all the way north to Castle Junction. It varies in width alongside the road but speed limits are relatively low so it is perfect for intermediate cyclists. Beginners should stick to the area between Waimānalo Beach Park and Bellows Beach Park, as the path is separated from the road, and a little safer.

Makapu'u Beach Park
41-095 KALANIANA'OLE HIGHWAY

Makapu'u Beach Park is a wide picturesque beach located directly below the lookout point. It is known as a good body boarding and body surfing beach. Care should be taken due to a strong undertow and rip currents. During the summer months when the seas are calm, snorkeling and diving are great along the side of the mountain cliff. Winter can bring huge crashing waves that create a pounding shore break, which makes conditions dangerous for anyone in the water. Lifeguards are on duty year round so it is a good idea to check with them for the current conditions. Facilities in this forty-seven-acre park include parking, picnic tables, BBQs, showers, and restrooms.

Kaupō Beach Park
41-401 KALANIANA'OLE HIGHWAY

Located across the road from Sea Life Park, this eight-acre beach park takes its name from the twenty-five-thousand-year-old Kaupō lava flow in the area. This beach is known by many different names depending on whom you are talking to. Some popular names include Kumu Cove, Baby Makapuʻu, and Cockroach Bay. No matter what the name, swimming is an excellent year round activity here due to the calm waters and sandy bottom that extend out one quarter mile from the shore's edge. The "Rabbit Island" surf break is accessible from here. Waves are best during Kona winds in the fall and winter, although the break is almost a mile offshore so be prepared to paddle. Or you could hitch a ride on a fisherman's boat departing from the Makai Pier nearby. The surf break is on the northwest side of the island. One word of caution: sharks are known to frequent this area. Parking, showers and restrooms are available. This area is frequented by homeless campers so stay towards the north end of the park.

Kaiona Beach Park
41-575 KALANIANAʻOLE HIGHWAY

Down the road a short way is Kaiona Beach Park, a small four-acre park. Kaiona means "sparkling waters" in Hawaiian and that is truly the case here. The shallow aquamarine waters allow you to see the rippling white sand on the bottom. The area is one of the few good snorkeling spots on the Windward Side when conditions are clear. Water runoff and trade winds can make the area murky and grey at times. At the southern end of the park is a spot known as Pāhonu Pond. Honu, the Hawaiian word for "turtle," were kept in the pond for the aliʻi (chiefs), so there was always a constant supply. The meat was forbidden to all commoners under penalty of death.

The park offers parking, restrooms, and showers. There is a small boat ramp located at the south end of the park that many locals use to launch small boats. Campers used to frequent this park, but it is no longer allowed.

Waimānalo Beach Park
41-741 KALANIANAʻOLE HIGHWAY

This seventy-five-acre beach park is located at the southern end of Waimānalo town. Its name means "potable water" which refers to the brackish water ponds located in the area that are used for irrigation. The wide strand of white beach beckons you to take a walk at water's edge. The relatively shallow water makes it a fun area for boogie boarding, body surfing, swimming, and fishing. Beware of the Portuguese man o' war (stinging jellyfish), as they are frequent visitors to these shores. Take a walk along the waterline before entering the water to see if any jellyfish have washed up on the shore. The man o' war looks like a transparent bubble with a long blue stinger hanging off the end of the bubble. The stings of these jellyfish are similar to bee stings; if you are stung, use vinegar and baking soda and rub on the affected area. Pouring human urine on the sting is a local antidote, but we suggest contacting the nearest lifeguard. This community park is heavily used on weekends with its abundance of sporting activities that take place on the athletic fields and basketball courts. There is plenty of parking and picnic tables are sprinkled throughout the grassy area under the trees and near the beach. Restrooms and showers are available here.

Access 17
LAUMILO STREET AT THE END OF WAILEA STREET

On a clear day Molokaʻi can be seen peeking behind the two islands just off the coast to the south. Ironwood trees provide afternoon shade and a nice backdrop to the beach. This access is just north of Waimānalo Beach Park and is connected by shoreline so it is less than a half mile to bathroom and showers at the park. The accesses are well marked in this area and a corresponding emergency access number is given for each of these accesses. The property lines are set back from the beach allowing a sandy path through the shade of ironwood trees from one end of Laumilo Street to the other. The 101B sign marks this access. For beginning bikers this stretch of the bike path along Kalanianaʻole Highway and Laumilo Street provides great scenery for an entertaining ride. It connects to the quiet neighborhood and passes through various arrays of architectural styles of homes in the neighborhood and then past the Waimānalo Polo Fields across Kalanianaʻole Highway before entering into Waimānalo Bay Beach Park and Bellows Field Beach Park.

Access 18
LAUMILO STREET AT THE END OF PU'UONE STREET

Just four houses down from access 17 and marked 101A, you will find more of this gorgeous stretch of beach. The beach is at least thirty feet wide allowing lots of area for sandcastle building as well as laying on the beach soaking up the sun's rays. As you proceed north the beach gets progressively wider between the beachfront houses and water's edge.

Access 19
LAUMILO STREET AT THE END OF 'ALA'IHI STREET

Look for the 100G sign for the entrance down a sandy path between a rock wall and a brick wall; soaring ironwood trees provide generous shady areas great for spreading a picnic blanket for a feast by the sea.

Access 20
LAUMILO STREET AT THE END OF MĀNANA STREET

Located at the 100F sign in between coral and moss rock walls this entrance passes a vacant lot on the left. There are a few ironwoods and palm trees to set up under near the vacant lot. Numerous shorefront homes have their catamarans parked on the upper beach ready to take advantage of the windy shores.

Access 21
LAUMILO STREET AT THE END OF HILU STREET

Plumeria trees almost block the 100E sign that marks the path to the beach. Kayakers and stand up paddle boarders were seen here so it could be a good launching point.

Access 22
LAUMILO STREET AT THE END OF KAʻULU STREET

The 100D sign marks this access, which looks like you are passing through a private yard to the beach. The beach is just as breathtaking from this access as it is from all the others although there are fewer trees beachside. To the left of the access there is a rope swing for keiki to play on.

Access 23
LAUMILO STREET AT THE END OF HĪNĀLEA STREET

Between a lava rock wall and chain-link fence this shady access marked 100C is similar to the other accesses, with loads of white sand and shallow waters to enjoy with palm trees and ironwood trees as a backdrop. Grassy patches play host to log benches made from the fallen trees.

Access 24
LAUMILO STREET AT THE END OF HĪHĪMANU STREET

Passing through this tree-lined access marked 100B will lead you to the beach; there isn't much shade near the coastline but plenty of sun-worshipping sandy shoreline to enjoy.

Access 25
LAUMILO STREET AT THE END OF ʻEHUKAI STREET

This is the last and northernmost access on Laumilo Street marked by the 100A sign. There is a nice shady area under the ironwood trees perfect for a picnic along with a built-in wooden bench and rope swing to entertain the kids and more adventuresome adults. By car it is .5 miles from Waimānalo Bay Recreation Area or Sherwood Forest, where there are bathroom and shower facilities. To get there, go back out onto Kalanianaʻole Highway and take a right. A short drive east will bring you to the sign on the right side of the road for the park.

Waimānalo Bay Beach Park
41-1055 KALANIANA'OLE HIGHWAY

Waimānalo Bay Beach Park used to be part of Bellows Air Force Base. In 1966, seventy-six acres at the southern end of the base were transferred to the State of Hawai'i. Once the military left, this spot became popular for stripping stolen cars and other illegal activities. The gang that performed these activities was compared to Robin Hood and his Merry Men of England, so locals began calling the area Sherwood Forest or Sherwood's. This Waimānalo beach is the longest stretch of beach on O'ahu measuring over 5.5 miles long. Facilities include parking, restrooms, showers, and picnic tables. There are ten campsites located on the north end of the beach park, but there is no camping until further notice by the city and county.

Bellows Field Beach Park
41-043 KALANIANA'OLE HIGHWAY

This beach park is part of the Bellows Air Force Base and is only available to the public on the weekends and national holidays. The base is used for active training during the week and a section of it is reserved for rest and recreation for the military. The public section is located between two streams. The two streams as well as the beach provide great fishing opportunities. There is a wide white sand beach perfect for sunbathing and the ocean provides excellent body boarding and body surfing due to a sand bar located just off shore. In addition to the resident Portuguese man o' war, other creatures include the pūpū pani, a small purple corkscrew-shaped snail and the ala eke, a crab better known as a sand turtle. The ala eke feed on the jellyfish and if threatened will burrow in the sand. Camping is allowed on weekends with permits available through the City and County of Honolulu.

Waimānalo History

Despite the pristine beauty of these beaches, Waimānalo has escaped commercial development and maintained its country atmosphere. The valley has a long history of agricultural use dating back to pre-European exploration. At one point the area was used for cattle ranching, but it gave way to sugar cultivation and the inception of the Waimānalo Sugar Company. When the sugar industry declined the valley became the center of diversified agriculture including corn, spinach, arugula, peppercress, asparagus and sea greens, along with many landscape plants. A large part of the area is Hawaiian homestead lands whose leases are awarded to native Hawaiians. The Territory of Hawai'i set the lands aside after Prince Jonah Kūhiō Kalaniana'ole authored the Hawaiian Homes Commission Act of 1920 to address the awarding of the Kings' former lands.

Directly across from Waimānalo Bay Beach Park are the polo fields. Polo games are held during the months of May through October at 2:30 on Sunday afternoons. With a modest $3.00 entrance fee for adults and free parking there is plenty of shade for picnicking. The family can enjoy a day out watching the polo games with ample time to swim at the beach across the street.

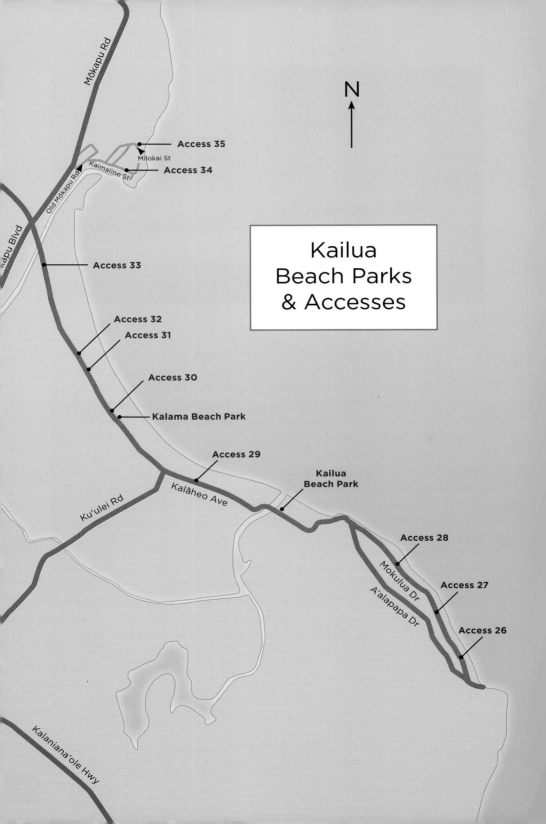

N

Kailua
Beach Parks
& Accesses

Mōkapu Rd

Old Mōkapu Rd

Kaimalino St

Milokai St

Access 35

Access 34

...pu Blvd

Access 33

Access 32

Access 31

Access 30

Kalama Beach Park

Access 29

Kuʻulei Rd

Kalāheo Ave

Kailua
Beach Park

Access 28

Mokulua Dr

Aʻalapapa Dr

Access 27

Access 26

Kalanianaʻole Hwy

KAILUA
Beach Parks and Accesses 26 to 35

Kailua is located on the windward or eastern side of Oʻahu. Kailua, meaning "two seas" or "two currents," is named for the two currents in Kailua Bay. The 2.5-mile beach, which borders it, is between Alāla and Kapoho Points. In 1988 coastal expert Dr. Stephen Leatherman, also known as Dr. Beach, ranked Kailua Beach as the best American beach.

Kalama Beach Park and Kailua Beach Park are two recreation areas that serve this community. Although bathrooms, showers, and phone booths are available at both, Kailua Beach Park has picnic tables and lifeguards. Lanikai Beach is south of Kailua Beach and is not adjoined by a public park, but Kailua Beach Park is only a tenth of a mile away from its northern end. Dr. Beach ranked Lanikai Beach as the best American beach in 1996. Lanikai's stunning coastline is accessible through accesses 26, 27, and 28. Additional entryways fall between the PROWs (Public Rights of Way) allowing access to Lanikai Beach every tenth of a mile. There are additional entryways between Kailua Beach PROWs as well, though they are not as frequent. The one drawback to these award-winning beaches is the presence of Portuguese man o' war jellyfish that often drift in, providing dinner for mole crabs, but painful stings for the unwary visitor. When present, you can see the poisonous blue and clear shiny tentacles on the shore. Immune to the venom, crabs will snag the spaghetti-like strings and wind them around their legs before dragging them under the sand and gobbling them up.

To get there from Honolulu, take H1 west to H3. Get off H3 at the Kāneʻohe/Kailua exit ramp. Take a right and follow Kāneʻohe Bay Drive. To get to the two northern accesses, 35 and 36, take a left on Mōkapu Road. For the eight remaining accesses, you will stay on Kāneʻohe Bay Drive, which becomes North Kalāheo Avenue after intersecting Mōkapu Road. You can also take the Pali Highway and Likelike Highway to get to Kailua. We suggest taking H3 because the panoramic vista of Kāneʻohe Bay as you exit the Koʻolau Mountain tunnel never fails to amaze. To get there by bus from downtown, take the 57 Bus Route to Kailua-Keolu. In Kailua, transfer to the 70 shuttle bus for Lanikai and Maunawili to get to the two northernmost accesses and exit at ʻAikahi Park shopping center. Take a short walk on Mōkapu Road about .5 miles to reach accesses 34 and 35.

This area is perfect for a biking adventure to explore all the accesses. Kailua is a bike friendly community with a recent addition of two solar-powered bike stations sponsored by the City and County of Honolulu. There are seven bikes available to rent with the use of a credit card; the bikes can be used on the nearby bike paths and are free for the first half hour. Rates vary for the amount of time used and the bikes can be returned at any bike station. The first two locations are at Uluniu Street in front of Formaggio and on Hekili Street in front of Boots and Kimo restaurant. There are miles of bike paths that start in Lanikai with many potential picnic spots along the way. The trail continues through the neighborhoods of Kailua town all the way to Mōkapu Road and the relatively isolated accesses 35 and 36.

Access 26
MOKULUA DRIVE AND LANIPŌ DRIVE

At the southern tip of Lanikai Beach, this ocean entry is located at the intersection of Lanipō Drive and Mokulua Drive. At high tide the waves are at the edge of this twenty-foot by twenty-foot sandy area. We watched kayakers congregate here, then paddle their way across the ocean to the Mokulua Islands, "moku" meaning island and "lua" meaning two. The larger island is Moku Nui and the smaller, Moku Iki. They are state bird sanctuaries and daytime access is allowed only at Moku Nui. The island is very popular with local seafarers in motorboats or kayaks. At high tide, waves break against the seawalls on both the north and south sides of this PROW. Both Lanakai and Kailua Beach are protected by an outside reef, making it one of the safest ocean currents in Hawai'i. This access is an excellent spot for kayakers and catamarans to explore their skills. There are some small surf breaks located a short paddle off shore. With big rubber boots, rod and bucket, a fisherman prepared to go wading along the outside seawall. Chances are this is a great place to fish at high tide. When we asked, he said there was a thin strip of beach here at low tide.

Access 27
MOKULUA DRIVE BETWEEN A'ALA DRIVE AND ONEKEA DRIVE

This right of way is a stone pier with stairs leading down to the shoreline. There is no beach at high tide. Boats moored in the shallow water led us to believe that locals often use accesses 26 and 27 as entries for sea vessels.

Access 28
MOKULUA DRIVE AND KAIOLENA DRIVE

This access is at the northern end of a mile-long white sandy beach. Lanikai's turquoise waters, pristine, wide beach, and swaying coconut palms make it one of the most picturesque areas on O'ahu. The protective offshore reef provides ideal swimming and snorkeling conditions, and green sea turtles can often be spotted here. Kayaks and catamarans available to rent crowd the shore. Other popular activities include outrigger canoeing, sailing, surfing, and windsurfing. This spot is a popular beach wedding site. Permits must be obtained from the state to avoid heavy fines. Lanikai Beach truly lives up to its meaning of a "heavenly sea."

Kailua Beach Park
526 KAWAILOA ROAD

With ample parking, shade trees, and a wide 2.5-mile long strip of sandy beach, this thirty-acre park was named the best beach in the USA in 1998 by *Conde Nast* Magazine. Kailua Beach Park is known for its excellent windsurfing conditions. Protected by an outer reef, the currents are among the safest on O'ahu. Kayaks, catamarans, and small boats line the beach. Other popular activities are swimming, kite boarding, snorkeling, fishing, and there are even a few surf breaks for beginners. The fine coral sand makes great sandcastles, and the University of Hawai'i's School of Architecture holds their annual sandcastle-building contest here. This park has lifeguards, picnic tables, and showers. There is a boat harbor at the south end of the park at Alāla Point and kayaks are available for rent across the street at the canal edge.

Access 29
SOUTH KALĀHEO STREET AND KU'UNIU STREET

Parking is on Ku'uniu Street, four-tenths of a mile to Kalama Beach Park, the nearest public facilities. This access is much like the other accesses with white sandy shores leading up to the inviting turquoise blue waters.

Kalama Beach Park
248 NORTH KALĀHEO AVENUE

Ironwood trees canopy this well shaded park, creating a welcome retreat from the afternoon sun. The roomy wooden structure sitting between the beach and the parking lot was the 1936 Boettcher home. The City and County of Honolulu bought this four-acre property in 1979 and it now serves as a community center. Developer Harold Castle named this area for Queen Kalama, wife of King Kamehameha III, who inherited Kailua in 1854 at her husband's death. In 1928, Castle set aside this section of Kailua Beach for the use of residents. When the City and County of Honolulu purchased the property, they renamed it Kalama Beach Park. Besides the community center, public amenities include parking, restrooms and showers. North of Kalama Beach Park, Kailua Beach is also called Castle Beach or Castles. The Castle family has owned a beachfront home at the end of the beach for many years. Mokolea Island or "Plover Island," a part of the Hawai'i State Seabird Sanctuary, can be seen off shore. Bodysurfing, body boarding, fishing, surfing, and windsurfing are all doable here.

Access 30
DUNE CIRCLE

Locally known as "Dune Beach Right of Way," this access is set between a green chain-link fence and a concrete block wall. Adjacent to Kalama Beach Club, it is less than .25 miles to access 31. You will need to park on Kapa'a Street, which is directly across from this access. Ironwood and palm trees provide shade on this sandy stretch.

Access 31

This beach entry is between a concrete block wall and a chain-link
fence. The access is at the midpoint
of Kailua Beach. There is no nearby
shade. This beach is dotted with fun
lovers during the week, with heavier
traffic on the weekends. There is a
forty foot stretch of beach at high
tide. You will need to park on Palapu
Street.

Access 32
NORTH KALĀHEO AVENUE AND ʻAINONI STREET

Located on North Kalāheo Avenue, the PROW is between a wooden fence on
the south and an ivy covered stucco wall on the north. Artistic chrome work
adorns the top of the wall. Evergreen trees shade the southern side of this long
sandy path. The leafy canopy is a welcome attraction at this access. Parking is
on ʻAinoni Street. This is a popular spot for families with young children and
dogs. Swimming, boogie boarding, boating, canoeing, kayaking, and windsurfing are popular activities here. This wide sandy beach is several miles long.

Access 33
NORTH KALĀHEO AVENUE AND KAILUANA PLACE

Just .5 miles before ʻAikahi Park Center on Kalāheo Boulevard, this is the last access for the long expanse of Kailua Beach. Parking is available on Kailuana Place. Access is through two chain-link fences. Only .5 miles from access 32, the conditions here are similar.

Access 34
KAIMALINO STREET AND LAUNA ALOHA PLACE

From Mōkapu Road heading north, take a right at the "Y" on Old Mōkapu Road and then immediately turn right on Kaimalino Street. Set in a quiet well-maintained neighborhood of modern homes, there is plenty of street parking around this access. Walking past a naupaka bush east of the access and a stone wall on the west brings you to a breathtaking view of the long white expanse of Kailua Beach and beyond. There is a small beach, which is washed away at high tide. Turtles frequent this shallow bay and people fish with nets and buckets for baby goatfish here. At high tide, the beach is gone. Kayakers and boaters were observed in this quiet bay.

Access 35
MILOKAI PLACE

Nestled in a quiet cul-de-sac between the green tiled roof and red tiled roof of two modern styled homes, this access is easily missed because the sign is hidden in the trees. This entry leads to a forty-foot-wide sand beach. There is a sign posted by the Hawai'i Health Department warning of arsenic and lead in the sand: "Children must not eat the sand." This access may not be appropriate for small children and the elderly due to a shelf of very sharp coral just beyond the beach. You must walk about .25 miles along the shore to get to one very small access to the ocean, which may only be visible at low tide. You will see rock and concrete steps leading down to a sandy-bottomed area. There are several tubes inserted into the coral here where fishing rods can be attached. The occasional tree on the edge of someone's lawn is the only shade available. The upscale shoreline homes are without seawalls. This must be a great place to see the sun rise as this beach faces directly east.

Kailua History

The earliest Hawaiians are believed to have settled on Kailua's shores fifteen centuries ago. These ancient Hawaiians told legends of the Menehune, a tiny people who worked in nocturnal secret at Kawainui Marsh and of Mo'o, a demigod who took the shape of a large lizard that attracted fish. In 1795 King Kamehameha I conquered O'ahu and settled with his chiefs and warriors in Kawainui Marsh and other parts of Kailua. The large freshwater fishponds and saltwater ponds were an excellent resource.

Harold Kainalu Long Castle, the only child of James Bicknell Castle of the lucrative partnership Castle and Cooke purchased 9,200 acres in Kailua and Kāne'ohe in 1917. Kailua was a sleepy town of barely 3,000 in the 1940s when World War II created dramatic changes. Castle donated land for many churches and schools. A department store, a supermarket, and a bowling alley were built in the 1950s, but the four-lane Pali highway tunneling through the Ko'olau Mountains was the most dramatic change, as it provided much easier access to the town. By 1960, the population was up to 24,400. Castle Hospital opened in 1963. The population was 36,513 at the 2000 census.

Like other Honolulu bedroom communities, the residents of Kailua have expressed concern regarding future development in Kailua. Their concerns included condominium construction, traffic, crime, and the increasing population. The Kailua Urban Design Task Force was created in 1994 by the Kailua Chamber of Commerce with the hope of developing a vision for Kailua's central business district. Kailuans had a future vision; they saw a tree-shaded Main Street with unique boutiques and restaurants as a major pedestrian thoroughfare. They decided all further development would need to enhance Kailua as a hometown village. Take a look around Kailua and you will see that the task force has met with success.

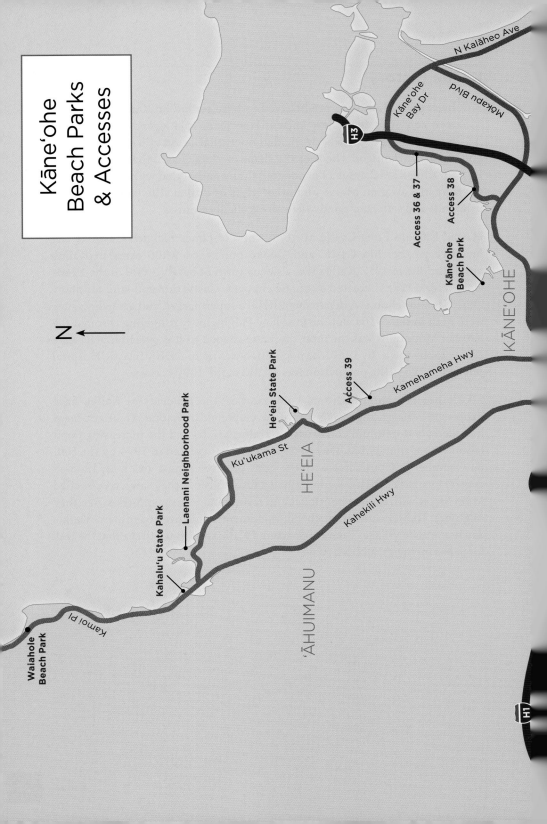

Kāne'ohe
Beach Parks
& Accesses

N ←

N Kalāheo Ave

Kāne'ohe
Bay Dr

Mōkapu Blvd

H3

Access 36 & 37

Access 38

Kāne'ohe
Beach Park

KĀNE'OHE

Access 39

Kamehameha Hwy

He'eia State Park

Ku'ukama St

HE'EIA

Laenani Neighborhood Park

Kahalu'u State Park

Kahekili Hwy

'AHUIMANU

Kamoi Pl

Waiahole
Beach Park

H1

KĀNEʻOHE
Beach Parks and Accesses 36 to 39

The name Kāneʻohe is taken from a Hawaiian legend about a woman who named her husband Kāneʻohe or "bamboo man" because his cruelty was compared to the sharp edge of cutting bamboo. Kāneʻohe Marine Corps Base borders the accesses to the south and Waiāhole Beach Park to the north. This area is very limited in access to the bay, and the beaches are poor to non-existent. The extraordinary views across the bay make it more suitable for picture taking, fishing, and boating. We have not listed the beaches on Kāneʻohe Marine Corps Base, as they are not open to the public.

By car, take Kalākaua Boulevard east to Kapahulu Avenue and turn left. Continue on Kapahulu under the freeway and veer left onto Waiʻalae Avenue and the entrance to H1 east. Continue on H1 freeway from Honolulu to 63 Likelike Highway east to Kāneʻohe. When you enter Kāneʻohe, Likelike Highway changes to Kāneʻohe Bay Drive; the first two accesses are located on this street. The remaining access and beach parks are off of Kamehameha Highway and can be reached by turning left off of Likelike Highway.

To reach the accesses by bus you would take the 56 or 85 Express Bus Routes from Ala Moana Shopping Center. There are no designated bike paths through this area but it can easily be explored by riding along the established roads.

Access 36 and 37
KĀNEʻOHE BAY BEACH REMNANT
KĀNEʻOHE BAY DRIVE B

These two accesses are connected. Access 37 leads from Kāneʻohe Bay Drive to the water, while access 36 is the actual waterfront access. Parking is located on the right side of Kāneʻohe Bay Drive in front of the Yacht Club Knolls development. The access is visible on the left side of the road. This tree-lined grassy path is about ten feet wide and leads to the bay. The bay is shallow and marshy

with many roots sticking up from the mud. The picturesque view of Kāne'ohe Bay with the Ko'olau Mountains as a backdrop is stunning, like something you would see in a movie. There are no beach or water activities other than possible fishing.

Access 38

This is one of the few accesses we could not locate. Even after checking through the tax key map, Googling the address and speaking to state workers who were in the area surveying, we were unable to locate the exact location. The City and County recently updated their access list and this access was omitted.

Kāne'ohe Beach Park
45-015 WAIKALUA ROAD

From Kamehameha Highway head north; turn right on Waikalua Road just after the library. Follow the road one mile to where it dead-ends into the park. Old

junky boats were scattered about the area and numerous dinghies were tied up to offshore moors. Most of Kāne'ohe Bay has been altered from its original state by dredging and landfill activities. Nearby is one of the few remaining fishponds called Waikalua Loko. The area is used as a community education site teaching ancient Hawaiian culture. One of the few parks fronting Kāneʻohe Bay, this park offers parking, restrooms, picnic tables, a playground structure, and showers, but little in the way of swimming activities. There is a boat launching area with a parking lot that is closed from 8 PM until 5 AM.

Access 39
IPUKA STREET

On Kamehameha Highway pass Windward Mall and cross Lilipuna Street. Proceed .6 miles to Ipuka Street. Take a right just after passing King Intermediate School. The access is located two houses down from Ipuka Place on the left. A local resident directed us to the access because the public right of way sign has been removed. There is just a pole sticking up with no sign on it. He claimed there was controversy in the neighborhood due to the blockage of the access site. There is a concrete sidewalk that leads down to the bay but it is overgrown with bushes and ends at a block wall that is at the water's edge at high tide. There is no beach, although we were told it is a great access to launch kayaks.

Heʻeia State Park
46-465 KAMEHAMEHA HIGHWAY

Located at the tip of Kealohi Point this park affords spectacular views of Kāneʻohe Bay and the offshore islands. The park's main feature is the Heʻeia Fishpond used by ancient Hawaiians for a constant supply of fish for royalty. There are paths that lead around the shaded grounds to the fishpond and a hula mound. Fishing is the preferred activity, so don't look to go swimming here. There is parking, restroom, and picnicking facilities, pay phone, and native Hawaiian plants display. There is also a hall available for rent on weekends administered by the Friends of Heʻeia State Park. The park closes at 6:45 PM and opens at 7 AM.

Laenani Neighborhood Beach Park

Continuing along Kamehameha Highway turn right on Laenani Drive and go .25 miles. This is another beach park on Kāneʻohe Bay that does not have a beach appropriate for swimming. The ocean off this small park is shallow reef more appropriate for fishing or picnicking, although there is a ramp that looks like it could be a boat launch area.

There is a lighted asphalt basketball court and picnic table with a large grassy area and a backstop for baseball games. There are restrooms, showers, and parking available here. Park is closed to the public from 9 PM to 5 AM.

Kahalu'u Regional Park

This undeveloped park is on the right on Kamehameha Highway just after the intersection of Kamehameha Highway and Kahikili Highway. There is a small boat launch, outrigger canoe storage and Porta Potties. The water is shallow and brown since it is next to the outlet of Waiola Stream.

Waiāhole Beach Park

Waiāhole Beach Park is located on Kamehameha Highway just past Waiāhole Valley Road. Waiāhole Beach Park's claim to fame is as a shooting location for the *Lost* TV series. The large grassy area of this undeveloped park served as the base camp for filming at the Waikāne Pier off shore. This beach park is a favorite of fishermen for the prized āholehole fish. There is a small narrow beach here with the ocean bottom being shallow reef. The two- to three-foot wide beach is brown sand and muddy. There are extraordinary views of China Man's Hat and the neighboring boat pier. The park is closed to the public from 10 PM to 5 AM. There are no public facilities of any kind.

Kāne'ohe History

The area has been an agricultural area since ancient Hawaiian times. Sugar was produced in the valley until the beginning of World War II. Now the crop of choice is bananas. The Kāne'ohe Marine Base located on Mōkapu Peninsula also played a vital part of World War II, with the first Japanese bombs being dropped there. Prior to World War II, the Navy and the Army claimed the area, when it was named Fort Hase. The Mōkapu Peninsula has been developed by the military for use as an air base complete with runways, hangers, operational and support facilities and some housing. There are two hills that are largely undeveloped and some ponds left for bird conservation. Beaches on the peninsula are open only to military personnel.

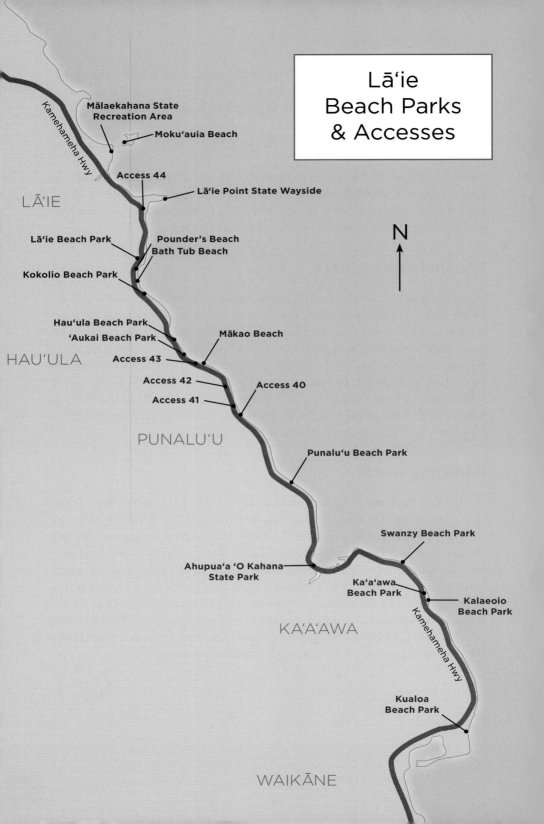

Lāʻie
Beach Parks
& Accesses

N

Kamehameha Hwy

Mālaekahana State
Recreation Area

Mokuʻauia Beach

Access 44

Lāʻie Point State Wayside

LĀʻIE

Lāʻie Beach Park

Pounder's Beach
Bath Tub Beach

Kokolio Beach Park

Hauʻula Beach Park

ʻAukai Beach Park

Mākao Beach

HAUʻULA

Access 43

Access 42

Access 41

Access 40

PUNALUʻU

Punaluʻu Beach Park

Swanzy Beach Park

Ahupuaʻa ʻO Kahana
State Park

Kaʻaʻawa
Beach Park

Kalaeoio
Beach Park

KAʻAʻAWA

Kamehameha Hwy

Kualoa
Beach Park

WAIKĀNE

LĀʻIE
Beach Parks and Accesses 40 to 44

The name Lāʻie is derived from two Hawaiian names meaning ʻie leaf. ʻIe ʻie is a type of climbing screw pine. There is no lack of trees along this stretch of Kamehameha Highway from Kualoa Beach Park to Lāʻie. This highway is one of the most scenic parts of the island as you wind along the coast through overgrown jungle foliage many shades of emerald green and past aqua blue waters speckled with darker colors of reef and sand. It is laced with pullouts and beach parks lining the eastern side of the highway. The ocean is shallow with only two- to twelve-foot depths extending at least .5 miles offshore. There are a number of beach parks that dot the coastline with restroom and shower facilities and ample parking. The first three accesses are mere extensions of a city park named Kaluanui.

To reach these accesses from Waikīkī take Kalākaua Boulevard east to Kapahulu, turn left. Follow Kapahulu under the freeway and veer left on to Waiʻalae Avenue. Stay in the center lane to enter H1 east. Take the 63 Likelike Highway toward Kāneʻohe, after exiting the tunnels take the 83 Kahekili Highway north.

By bus from Ala Moana Shopping Center, take the Route 55 Kāneʻohe/Circle Island bus.

For experienced cyclists, start your ride at Kualoa Beach Park following Kamehameha Highway. There is a small shoulder on the road to ride on. Past Lāʻie town there is a bike path removed from the road on the left side. It fronts fields with horse and cows and sweeping views of the Koʻolau Mountains behind. Speed limits are low along this stretch of highway but care should be taken when riding with traffic. There are plenty of places to stop along the way for a quick dip in the ocean to cool off, or enjoy a picnic on the beach.

Kualoa Beach Park
49-479 KAMEHAMEHA HIGHWAY

The views at this park are nothing short of stunning. The rich green mountains just above Kualoa Ranch provide the backdrop for the sparkling turquoise waters and Mokoliʻi or Chinaman's Hat Island located just offshore. The name Kualoa means "long ancestral background" which is fitting because ancient Hawaiians considered this area sacred. Whale bones washed up on the beaches here and the fertility god "Lono" was associated with the area. The aliʻi's (chief's) children were schooled here. The story of Mokoliʻi Island says that it is part of the tail of the moʻo dragon named Mokoliʻi. Pele's younger sister, Hiʻiaka (the goddess of bright light) was on a trip to visit her family on the North Shore and she encountered the lizard dragon. She fought Mokoliʻi with spears of lightning and sliced off its tail and threw it into the ocean where it landed just off shore. The islet is also known as Chinaman's Hat because the shape is reminiscent of the hats worn by Chinese plantation workers. There are many paintings of the island in local galleries, depicting a Chinese man sitting just underneath the water with his

head down and the hat just above water. In 1972, this site was chosen as the launching point for the *Hōkūleʻa*, a replica of the original Polynesian canoes used to travel to Hawaiʻi. In its honor, a part of the beach has been renamed Hōkūleʻa Beach.

This park is almost 150 acres and although there is very little beach for swimming, there is a huge expanse of grass for picnicking. The beach park provides parking with restrooms, showers, and public phones. There are plenty of picnic tables and barbeque pits. Camping is allowed on weekends at the southern end of the park with permits obtained from the city and county. Fishing and kayaking are popular activities. There is access to Mokoliʻi Island by snorkeling

and walking in the shallow water at low tide but care should be taken because of strong ocean currents. As with other windward shores, Portuguese man o' war can be found in the waters due to on-shore breezes. Lifeguards are on site daily during the months of June through August and only on weekends during the other months of the year.

Kalaeō'io Beach Park

Continuing on Kamehameha Highway, just after the bridge over Ka'a'awa stream is Kalaeō'io Beach Park. The beach park is located across from Ka'a'awa Place and is on the southern end of Ka'a'awa Beach Park. This undeveloped beach park offers snorkeling and picnicking activities. Swimming is poor due to seasonal high surf. There are no lifeguards or facilities at this beach park.

Ka'a'awa Beach Park
51-392 KAMEHAMEHA HIGHWAY

There is a reef off shore that protects this beach park, making the waters generally calm and safe for swimming. The beach is narrow but has nice white sand. Snorkeling is good here for experienced swimmers as the currents are strong. Lifeguards are only on duty during the summer months June through August. Facilities at this two-acre park include parking, showers, telephone, restrooms, and picnic tables.

Swanzy Beach Park
51-369 KAMEHAMEHA HIGHWAY

Swanzy Beach Park is a five-acre stretch of beach that was donated by Julia Judd Swanzy to the City and County of Honolulu to create a park. The park, which was created in the 1920s, took its name from the benefactor and was called Julia Judd Swanzy Park until the 1950s when the name was shortened to Swanzy Beach Park. The facilities at the park

include parking, restrooms, a playground, basketball courts, baseball field, and picnic tables. Camping is no longer available until further notice. There is little beach here to be enjoyed and a seawall was built to prevent further erosion. The beach is completely submerged at high tide. Fishing, squid, and octopus hunting would be a preferred activity here because the ocean bottom is strewn with rocks that provide many hiding places for creatures. Swimming is not recommended.

Ahupuaʻa ʻO Kahana State Park
55-222 KAMEHAMEHA HIGHWAY

Kahana Bay is a beautiful quiet beach park nestled at the mouth of the bay.

This park is part of a land division that runs from the mountain to the sea, known as an ahupuaʻa. This is the only public ahupuaʻa on the island and worth exploring if you are interested in seeing some of Hawaiʻi's earliest dated remains. The families that live there are part of the personnel that keep the history and culture alive. The remains of the Huilua Fishpond are just south of the park about .25 miles. Hawaiian legend has it that the pond was built by menehune, small people who worked at night to complete building projects. Numerous tsunamis since the early 1920s have damaged it but there are plans for restoration. In the 1800s, the valley was host to a train line that ran between Kahana Plantation and the Kahuku sugar mill. Later, the U.S. military used the valley for jungle training.

There are hiking trails that lead back into the valley from the main parking area. White sandy beach makes for easy entry to the water, and small children can safely play near the water's edge. The bay is perfect for kayaking, swimming, fishing, body boarding, and stand up paddle boarding. The bay is also known for the seasonal visit of the akule fish, along with pāpio, and goatfish. The snorkeling is not too good here due to Kahana Stream emptying into the bay. One word of caution, as beautiful as this lush beach park is, it can easily be spoiled by attacks of mosquitoes. So be sure to wear plenty of mosquito repellent if you plan on spending any time here. Facilities include Porta Potti bathrooms, showers (when they are turned on), picnic tables, camping sites, and parking.

Punaluʻu Beach Park
53-309 KAMEHAMEHA HIGHWAY

Just north of Kahana Bay is Punaluʻu Beach Park. There was once a fishpond located here in Punaluʻu, hence the name's meaning of "spring dived for." The beach park is lined with coconut palms and ironwood trees that provide afternoon shade. There are picnic tables, restrooms, showers, and public phones here. The north end of the beach has a grassy area under the trees leading up to the beach perfect for an afternoon picnic. A reef off shore provides snorkeling, although it can be windy, which makes the water cloudy and visibility poor. There are no lifeguards at this beach.

Access 40
Kaluanui Beach

A few miles after passing through Punaluʻu in the 53-600 block there is a sign identifying the park as Kaluanui Beach, although there are no facilities here only a water fountain. The ocean is shallow and sandy with little reef, for ideal swimming conditions most of the year. There is a small patch of grassy area with ironwood trees between the road and the beach, which provides a nice spot for picnicking. To the south there is a neighborhood of houses fronting the ocean, but the beach is impassable at high tide as the water washes right up to the seawalls. To the north, is a nice walk along the beach, although it is also nearly washed up at high tide. Access 41 can be reached by taking the short walk northward.

Access 41
Kaluanui

This access is a short .25 miles up the road. Parking is along the shoulder of Kamehameha Highway but there are no signs that designate the area as a park or as a public right of way. Look for the small yellow sign with 28B located just across the street from Pūhuli Street and the bus stop. This area is nice for swimming although we spotted Portuguese man o' war and small pebbles strewn up on the beach.

Access 42
Kaluanui

We never found the exact location of the access. It is in the general area of Sacred Falls Park (now closed to the public) located on Kamehameha Highway. The beach is impassable in both directions at high tide as the ocean splashes up on the seawalls of the adjacent homes, immersing the flat sandy beach. The water is shallow with reef that makes for good snorkeling or swimming.

Mākao Beach

This beach is separated from the road by some concrete pylons. There is a narrow pull-off for cars to park alongside the road. A shallow reef is located off shore, which make it an excellent snorkeling spot. Near the north end of the pull-off there is a narrow high spot on the sand to park your things. At high tide the beach almost disappears and the waters can be cloudy if the trade winds are blowing hard. The nearest facilities are located down the road at Hauʻula Beach Park.

Access 43
Hauʻula Beach Remnant

The access is on Kamehameha Highway across from Hauʻula Homestead Road but there is no parking directly in front. Parking is allowed just south of the access on the shoulder of the road and the beach is easily accessed from the road. The access itself is colorful, with the barn red houses sandwiching the pathway to the quiet bay beyond. The houses are quaint older beach shacks resting on foundations that reach right up to the high water mark. This is a beautiful spot to relax under some large trees and take a swim in the shallow sandy-bottom ocean. There is a stream opening to the south that runs into the ocean during storms, cutting off the houses from the beach directly in front of the parking area.

ʻAukai Beach Park
54-071 KAMEHAMEHA HIGHWAY

Aukai Beach Park is located just north of Hauʻula Elementary School at an estuary end of a stream. There are no facilities here just a pull-off area on the beach side with some trees and grass. The beach is covered with smooth black pebbles making entry for swimming a challenge, although it makes a nice fishing spot. There are no facilities here, but just to the north is Hauʻula Beach Park.

Hauʻula Beach Park
54-135 KAMEHAMEHA HIGHWAY

Located directly across from the Lanakila Church in Hauʻula town, this beach park offers grassy fields leading up to a narrow beach. There is parking available in various pull-offs in the three-foot-high concrete block wall fronting the park. Handicapped parking is available in front of a pavilion with restrooms, showers, and public phone. The beach is about thirty feet wide and fronts a shallow reef which provides protection for swimmers, snorkelers, and fishermen. Body boarders and beginning surfers can be spotted at the north end of the beach, where there is a small break. Lifeguards are on duty from June through August. Camping is allowed here with a permit obtained from the city and county.

Kokololio Beach Park
55-017 KAMEHAMEHA HIGHWAY

This beach park begins with a stretch that winds along Maloʻo bay. The beaches from south to north are Kokololio, Mahʻakea Beach, and Bath Tub Beach, and then a limestone point prevents you from accessing the northern end of the bay. So you will have to go back to the road and drive to Pounder's Beach and Lāʻie Beach Park.

Kokololio Beach Park offers parking, restrooms, showers, and picnic tables. Mountains hugging the coastline with ironwood trees on the beach form the backdrop for this beautiful bay. Camping is allowed here with permits obtained from the city and county. The beautiful white sandy beach is suitable for swimming in the summer months. During the winter, the waves begin to pound on the shore and some boogie boarding and surfing is available to the more experienced water person. Fishing is available year round.

Bath Tub Beach

Located at the northern end of Kokololio Beach Park, Bath Tub Beach is so called because a natural reef wall forms a barrier for a protected swimming area no deeper than five feet at high tide. This makes for warm, calm waters suitable for swimming and wading. Outside the wall snorkelers will be delighted with the variety of ocean life. No lifeguards are on duty.

Pounder's Beach Park
55-205 KAMEHAMEHA HIGHWAY
SOUTH END OF LĀ'IE BEACH PARK

This beach was named for the pounding shore break that surfers and body boarders are attracted to. There is a shallow sandbar that somewhat protects the inner swimming area, but in the winter it produces dangerous wave conditions and rip currents. Swimming is only recommended during the calmer summer months. Fishing, surfing, and boogie boarding are other activities to engage in at this park. Unfortunately, there are no restroom facilities here, only showers.

Lā'ie Beach Park
55-205 KAMEHAMEHA HIGHWAY

Many locals are attracted to this beach for the safe swimming and beginner surfing, and boogie boarding breaks located directly in front of the parking lot. The ample lot provides parking for forty-one cars. Three picnic tables line the grass and showers are located nearby. Trees shade the beach, and Kōloa Stream terminates at the ocean here. To the north of the beach are the remnants of a boat dock for Lā'ie Landing. There are no facilities here.

Access 44
LĀ'IE- KAMEHAMEHA HIGHWAY

Continuing on Kamehameha Highway .5 miles from Polynesian Cultural Center and .1 miles from the BYU Hawai'i Campus Sign is access 44. Its sign is designated as emergency response Location 20A. Here is another hidden treasure! This tranquil beach extends at least a mile southward and about one quarter mile northward. Snorkeling, swimming, kayaking, and fishing all would be great activities here. Although the beach was not deserted, everyone we met along the way was friendly. A short walk to the north ends at a promontory with houses dotting the cliffs above. During low tide the beach is about twenty feet wide but much of that is swallowed up at high tide. The walk southward is peaceful and scenic, although it was strewn with rubbish and driftwood washed up on the shore, probably due to a storm drain outlet further

south. We came across a WWII bunker left sitting on the beach. Beyond the bunker, the beach is washed away, but there is a protected area for snorkeling fronted by a coral reef that is accessible at low tide.

Lāʻie Point State Wayside

Just a couple hundred yards north on Kamehameha Highway turn right at the first stop light onto ʻAnemoku Street. Follow the road and make a right turn at the "T" on to Naupaka Street. At the end of the road there is a small parking area and a memorial stone noting the legend surrounding this promontory. The Hawaiian name for Lāʻie Point is Laniloa, which Hawaiian legend

says was a giant lizard standing upright ready to kill any intruder. He was confronted by Kana, a warrior. Kana was on a mission to kill all the lizards or mo'o on the island. Kana easily defeated Laniloa and cut him into five pieces, which he tossed off the coast. The results are the five tiny islands seen just off the point. The point affords a sweeping view of Lā'ie and the windward coast to the south, and Kukuiho'olua Island to the north. Kukuiho'olua is one of the five islands and is long, thin, and about twenty feet tall with an oval window hole in the center of the island. The area is a bird sanctuary with daytime access, but care should be taken if trying to get to the island, as ocean currents can be very strong here.

Mālaekahana State Recreation Area
56-335 KAMEHAMEHA HIGHWAY

This park is nestled in the trees right off Kalanai Point. There are full facilities here with nice restrooms, showers, and parking in a dirt parking lot. There are two sections of the park; the first parking area is for picnickers with picnic tables, fire pits, and showers under the trees. A large section of the hill fronting the beach is roped off due to being a wedge-tailed shearwater nesting area. The beach is narrow here but care should be taken when swimming due to cross currents. The second area for picnicking is located in front of the fenced maintenance yard. To the left of the restrooms is the picnic area and to the right is the camping area. There are showers, phones, and water fountains. This area is handicapped accessible with picnic tables provided to accommodate wheelchairs. An open grassy area is dotted with picnic tables and fire pits. Just beyond the trees is the beach, and access to Goat Island. The area is shallow at low tide and can be navigated to by walking (with reef shoes) or snorkeling. At high tide the beach is quite narrow and strewn with driftwood. The farthest area of the park is reserved for camping with permits obtained from the State. The campsites are in two sections, and protected from ocean breezes by a hill and trees. There are separate restrooms facilities for the campers with kitchen sink areas for clean up in addition to large restroom facilities. The beach is sandy and shallow, good for swimming or snorkeling.

Moku'auia Beach

Moku'auia, located just off the coast from Mālaekahana Beach Park, is better known as Goat Island. Access to the island is over the coral reef during low tide. Check to see what the tides and wave conditions are before trying to walk over. Be sure to return before the tide rises. Some people use flotation devices, rafts, kayaks, or boogie boards to help them make the passage to the island. The beach with the best conditions is on the leeward side of the tiny island, just to the left of the welcome sign. There is a gradual sloping sandy beach that is somewhat protected from the waves, which makes it a great place to swim.

Lā'ie History

Much of the modern day town of Lā'ie is owned by Hawai'i Reserves Inc., a holding company for the Mormon Church. They own the Polynesian Cultural Center as well as many commercial properties such as the shopping center and various residential properties.

Prior to the missionaries' arrival, Lā'ie was known as a Pu'uhonua or place of refuge. If a person had committed a crime or broken a rule they could flee to a Pu'uhonua and escape their pursuers. If their pursuers came into the Pu'uhonua the priests that resided there would kill them. The fugitives who stayed there were given two choices, one was to stay there for a while then enter the priesthood and assist in affairs of the Pu'uhonua or they could stay there a specific amount of time, then reenter society without fear of prosecution.

In 1865, the Mormon Church bought a "barren and windswept" land of what would later be the Polynesian Cultural Center, BYU Hawai'i Campus and the Hawai'i Temple, fulfilling the church's vision of becoming a missionary factor affecting thousands of people. Lā'ie was also well known for the hukilau they staged on the beach as fundraisers to rebuild a burnt-down church. Hukilau is a combination of two Hawaiian words meaning pull the net. Hukilau were celebrated with a feast after the fish were harvested from the nets. The hukilau ran from 1947 to 1971 when they were finally suspended. The area now known as Hukilau Beach is used as a private beach camp, but there are no facilities located there. In 1993, Hawai'i Reserves Inc. bought parts of Lā'ie and developed a master plan for the community. They are dedicated to expanding BYU and providing more housing and job opportunities at the Polynesian Cultural Center.

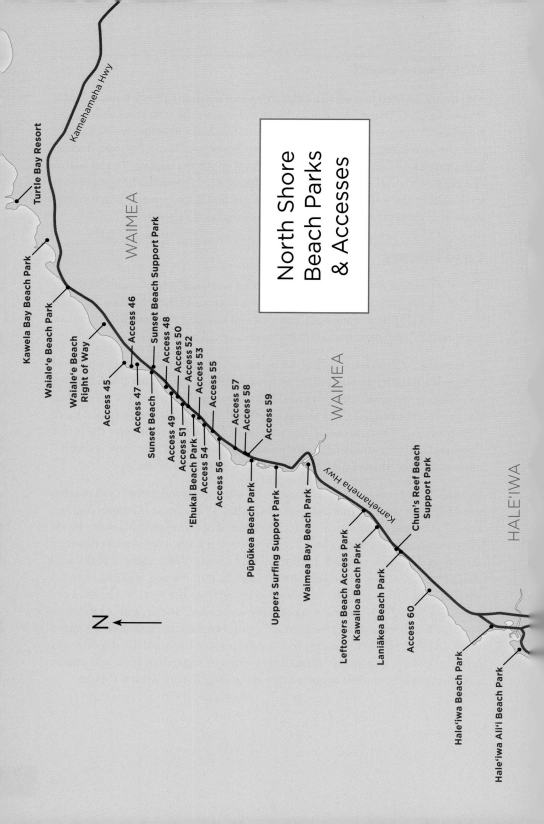

North Shore Beach Parks & Accesses

Kamehameha Hwy

Turtle Bay Resort

Kawela Bay Beach Park

Waiale'e Beach Park

Waiale'e Beach Right of Way

WAIMEA

Access 45

Access 46

Access 47

Sunset Beach

Sunset Beach Support Park

Access 48

Access 49

Access 50

Access 51

Access 52

Access 53

'Ehukai Beach Park

Access 54

Access 55

Access 56

Access 57

Access 58

Pūpūkea Beach Park

Access 59

Uppers Surfing Support Park

Waimea Bay Beach Park

WAIMEA

Kamehameha Hwy

Leftovers Beach Access Park

Kawailoa Beach Park

Chun's Reef Beach Support Park

Laniākea Beach Park

Access 60

Hale'iwa Beach Park

HALE'IWA

Hale'iwa Ali'i Beach Park

N

NORTH SHORE
Beach Parks and Accesses 45 to 60

The North Shore, affectionately called "Da Country," is free from large-scale commercial development along its rural coastline. Lush, jade mountainsides descend into crystal shores and aquamarine waters. The name Hale'iwa is a combination of two words meaning "house" or hale of the "frigate bird" or iwa. Hale'iwa town and the North Shore beaches have two distinctly different faces depending on the time of year you visit. In the winter, this is a surfer's mecca where thousands of fans and media follow internationally renowned surfers as they ride some of the world's largest waves. The Van's Triple Crown of Surfing hosts three "invitation only" surfing events at various beaches during November and December. The extremely crowded area has throngs of people venturing out to marvel at monster surf, and the fearless watermen and women. In the summer, it reverts to a sleepy little plantation town with art galleries, boutiques, restaurants, and oh so popular shave ice stores to pass the time. When the roaring waves are gone, flat calm waters prevail, ideal for diving, snorkeling, and swimming.

To get there from Honolulu, take Pali Highway or Likelike Highway through the mountains to Kamehameha Highway. Proceed north past the Lā'ie accesses and continue around the northeast tip of the island. For bus transportation take the Route 52 to Wahiawā-Circle Island. The accesses lie between Turtle Bay and Waimea Bay Beach Park, with several other public parks scattered in between. Accesses 45 to 56 are located on Kē Nui Road, a small access road between the beachfront homes and Kamehameha Highway.

A narrow asphalt bike path beginning at Sunset Beach and ending at Pūpūkea Beach Park makes for a leisurely ride with plenty of spots to stop and explore along the way. Intermediate bikers may be interested in continuing on past Sunset Beach along Kamehameha Highway. There are small shoulders to ride on and the speed limit is low so it is relatively safe.

Turtle Bay/Kawela Bay

Located at the northeastern tip of the island, the resort community provides public access to some of the most isolated spots on the island. Turtle Bay, Kawela Bay and the areas east of Turtle Bay that lead toward Kahuku can be reached by parking at the Turtle Bay Resort. From Kamehameha Highway turn right

on Kuilima Road, follow the road to the guard shack, and ask for a public access pass. The resort provides forty parking stalls for public use.

Turtle Bay Resort Beach, also known as Bayview Beach, is a beautiful cove complete with a beachside restaurant, snack bar, sandy beach, a sand volleyball court, snorkeling, and other beach activities. The area is immediately to the right of the hotel. There are two limestone reef shelves extending out from the beach, leaving this area somewhat protected from the North Shore surf. Numerous fishing spots along the reefs make shore casting popular. During the winter, rip currents can flow out of the bay making swimming unsafe. Experienced surfers paddle out of the cove to reach "Rainbows" and "Baggers" surf sites, which lie east of the resort. Care should be taken to avoid rocks and shallow spots in the area; there are no lifeguards on duty. In the summer's calm waters, swimming and snorkeling are preferred activities. Equipment rentals are at the snack bar, and restrooms and showers are available.

Venture farther to the east to a horse trail meandering through ironwood trees facing the shores. You will pass Kaihalulu Beach, a sandy cove that abuts the Turtle Bay Resort Golf Club. We observed a monk seal and her pup lounging in one of the many coves dotting this coastline. At the tip of Kahuku Point are views of Hanaka'ilio Beach to the east. Unfortunately, there is no road access to reach the remote beaches between here and Kahuku Beach (mentioned in Lā'ie section).

Kawela Bay is located to the west of the Turtle Bay Resort Hotel. A public access sign and path at the front of the hotel driveway leads to this quiet cove. Ironwood trees are a shady haven on the narrow white sand beach that extends for miles. Swimming, snorkeling, scuba diving, surfing, boogie boarding, stand up paddle boarding, and fishing are all enjoyable activities here. A reef that protects this cove from high winter surf makes for safe swimming most of the year. The western side of the cove is best for swimming because there are fewer reefs and rocks. There are a few surf breaks on the outer reef just outside the cove.

Waialeʻe Beach Park

Waialeʻe or "rippling water" is a narrow twenty-six-acre park located on Kamehameha Highway approximately 1.5 miles past the entrance to Turtle Bay (traveling from the east) between the highway and the ocean. Parking and portable toilets are the only amenities at this undeveloped beach park. A rocky shelf lines the white sandy beach, which fronts the park, and ironwood trees provide shade along the backshore. The beach is about twenty to thirty feet wide and is scattered with rocks and driftwood. Just to the left of the beach park is Kūkaʻimanini Island. The black coral rock and choppy waters make access to the island dangerous. In the summer when waters are calmer, snorkeling, fishing, diving and kayaking become possible. The surf site "Bongs" is on the reef off shore. There are no lifeguards on duty at this beach, so swimmers need caution.

Waialeʻe Beach Right of Way

Though not listed with the city and county, Honolulu acquired several adjacent beachfront lots at the end of a beach access road running through the Waialeʻe Livestock Center. The lots serve as a small park, and a white metal gate bars the driveway to the access, so you will need to park outside the gate. It is only a .25-mile walk to a grassy expanse bordering a rocky beach that becomes wider and sandier as you head west. A shallow reef fronts the beach, so swimming, boogie boarding, and surfing are all doable beyond the reef. The surf site "Revelations" is here. The water seemed a little rough in the winter, but is probably much calmer in the summer months. No public facilities of any kind.

Access 45
O'OPUOLA STREET AND
SUNSET POINT

From Kamehameha Highway this access is located just .2 miles from Sunset Beach Support Park on O'opuola Street, at the dead end. With only a couple of parking spots

next to the access, additional street parking is possible on other streets to the west. During the summer when the ocean is flat, a sandy pocket identified by an orange buoy marks a place to swim, windsurf, snorkel, paddle board, and kayak. The point is surrounded by an inviting coral reef, open for exploration during calm seas. Catamarans and kayaks often dot this sixty-foot-wide beach. Around the point is a cove with access to "Backyards" surf site; located on the right side of the cove and at the far end is "Velzyland." No public amenities.

Access 46
KAHAUOLA STREET

Kahauola Street is the first left turn after Sunset Beach Support Park. The access is located at the end of the road. A lava rock wall and ironwood trees line the entrance to this access. The access is only about .1 miles from the Oʻopuola Street access. The wide sandy beach has a rocky shore exposed at low tide. A swimming pocket is twenty feet to the west, in front of a concrete platform and a strange black plastic triangle popping out of the sand.

Access 47
HUELO STREET

Just 200 feet from access 46 and 100 feet from Sunset Beach is the most frequented public access on this end of Sunset Beach. Parking is very limited on Huelo Street, so park on surrounding streets. The access is clearly marked with a chain across the sandy lane to prohibit cars. A coral rock wall and chain-link fence marks the entrance. This seems to be a favorite spot of locals, as the ac-

cess was lined with bikes and strollers. A quaint picnic area with two picnic tables is set up under the shady trees. Diving, spear fishing, snorkeling, and swimming are favored activities during flat surf. Surfing and boogie boarding extend down to this area from Sunset Beach Park during high surf.

Sunset Beach Park and Sunset Beach Support Park
59-104 KAMEHAMEHA HIGHWAY

Sunset Beach Park is world famous for its waves and sunset views. The name Sunset Beach was coined in the 1920s when lots along the two-mile stretch between Sunset Point and Pūpūkea Beach Park were offered for sale. It was marketed as the Sunset Tract to highlight the area's splendid sunsets. In the late 1940s, Waikīkī surfers discovered the phenomenal waves while exploring for other surf spots. It became more popular in the 1950s when California surfers followed their local peers to these amazing breaks. When Sunset Beach was featured in several surfing movies and exposed to the international surfing community, its popularity soared. "Sunset" is now one of the most famous surf spots in the world and home to the O'Neil World Cup and Gidget Pro contests, part of the Van's Triple Crown of Surfing Contest, which began in 1983.

This white sand beach is among the finest on the island. The sandy shore gently slopes into the water in the summer, but becomes treacherous in the winter. In the summer, swimming and snorkeling are favorite activities, but you should still check with the lifeguards, as there can be dangerous rip currents. When winter rolls around this beach is better for sun tanning and being wowed by the surfers attempting to catch the fifteen- to twenty-foot waves. On the east end of the park is the surf site "Sunset." In early December, surf contests bring the world's best surfers to this beach. Sunset is best known as the starting point for the Triple Crown of Surfing contest. There are restrooms, showers, and phones located across the highway at the support park, and parking on both sides. This one-acre park provides plenty of trees, green grass and shade for a picnic to escape from the crowds across the street. Cold drink and snack vendors often frequent the park grounds.

Access 48
KĒ NUI ROAD

This is the eastern most access of the six accesses located on Kē Nui Road. Take the second right onto Kē Nui Road, after Sunset Beach Park from Kamehameha Highway. Parking is along the road next to the bike path. The entrance to this access is an asphalt road with a "24 hour no parking—tow away" sign painted on the road. Rows of ironwood trees make a cool canopy. Stairs lead to a wide sandy beach. A beach volleyball net is located on the beach. Near shore is a shallow rocky reef that provides snorkeling opportunities in calm seas. Swimming, fishing, and boogie boarding are popular activities here. No public facilities are available on Kē Nui Road accesses.

Access 49
KĒ NUI ROAD

To get to this access take the third right after Sunset Beach Park from Kamehameha Highway. Parking is on Kē Nui Road. This access is clearly marked as a right of way along with a yellow emergency response Location 279D posted at the entrance on Kē Nui Road. A paved private driveway with a vacant lot on the right dead-ends to a sandy path leading to a low lava rock wall. A shallow reef area directly fronts the access

in the winter. During the summer the sandy beach provides plenty of space for beach picnics and activities. Fishing, swimming, surfing, boogie boarding, and even small boats and catamarans were observed here.

Access 50
KĒ NUI ROAD

Located at the fourth entrance to Kē Nui Road from Sunset Beach, this right of way is .25 miles from the previous access. It is clearly marked with the blue PROW sign and yellow 279C emergency response sign. A dusty dirt path lined by wooden fences leads to a concrete stair descent to the widest section of beach on Kē Nui Road. There is a sandy-bottom area to swim or boogie board, and a reef in front provides snorkeling opportunities during the summer months. During the winter, surfers use this access as the entry point to "Gas Chambers" and "Kammieland" surf breaks, while photographers station themselves on the beach to catch the surfers in action.

Access 51
KĒ NUI ROAD

This entry to the beach is lined by trees and bushes and is about one hundred feet west from access 50. It is clearly marked with the access sign and 279B emergency access sign. There is a steep wall with a thirty-foot drop to the beach in the summer. There is no safe access down the beach wall, although we did see horseback riders riding among the trees. During the winter, sand is deposited on the beach to fill the steep drop-off and huge waves come right up to the access entrance.

Access 52
KĒ NUI ROAD

This access, easily spotted from Kē Nui Road, is directly across from a wooden utility pole and is clearly marked with a blue PROW sign and 279A emergency access sign. One hundred feet of wide sand beach is accessible via a grass path to access stairs. During the winter months the beach is swallowed up by ocean with the high water mark coming to within twenty feet of the access.

'Ehukai Beach Park
59-337 KĒ NUI ROAD

Better known as the "Banzai Pipeline" this beach park is another famous surf spot on the North Shore. Easily spotted on Kamehameha Highway, the park is directly across from Sunset Elementary School. During the winter, the waves form perfect barrels, which make for spectacular surf shows by pro surfers. The Billabong Pipeline Masters surf contest, the final jewel in the Van's Triple Crown of Surf event, is held here in mid-December. Many injuries are incurred here due to the powerful surf breaks on the shallow reef and sandbar, so lifeguards are on duty year round. During the summer when the sea is flat, swimming and snorkeling are popular activities. The small one-acre park is shaded by ironwoods, and provides parking for about fifty cars, restrooms, phones, showers, and picnic tables.

Access 53
KĒ NUI ROAD

This access is about .1 miles from 'Ehukai Beach Park. You can access it by continuing west on the one lane road that goes through the beach park. 278D is on the emergency access sign. Parking is limited to areas along the bike path or on Kamehameha Highway. Located right between two vine-covered stone walls is a dirt pathway to the access way. Concrete stairs lead down to a beach with several hundred feet of coarse white sand. A shallow water pool in the center of the beach is perfect for keiki, when surf is flat in the summer. Waves make this a dangerous spot during the winter, suitable for only the most experienced surfers. Boogie boarders should avoid this area, as it is an extension of the Banzai Pipeline.

Access 54
KAMEHAMEHA HIGHWAY

Parking for this beach entry is on Kamehameha Highway to the east. Located behind a 35 mph speed limit sign at the beginning of a six-foot-high lava rock wall paralleling Kamehameha Highway, the access is down a dirt path that leads to stairs. The left side of the stairs has eroded and is unsafe so stick to the right. There is a steep drop-off from sand to water. The huge waves come all the way to the property lines in the winter. Banzai surfers are easily viewed from here. During the summer there is a large berm of sand. Emergency access sign is labeled 278C.

Access 55
Banzai Rock Beach Support Park

Just after passing a pedestrian bridge on the right side of Kamehameha Highway, is Banzai Rock Beach Support Park. A dirt parking area abuts the road, but no other facilities are available. Also known as Ka Waena Beach, this is an undeveloped beach park located at the east end of Ka Waena Road. Lifeguards are on duty here to assist surf sites to the north and south. Surf sites on the north end are "Off-the-Wall" and "Backdoors." "Log Cabins" is to the south. A reef in front of the lifeguard towers allows for swimming and snorkeling in calmer summer months.

Access 56
KA WAENA ROAD

Designated as emergency access 278A, the access is off of Ka Waena Road, just past the intersection of Ka Waena Road with Kamehameha Highway. Ka Waena Road is a one-way road heading north towards Banzai Rock Beach Support Park. No facilities are available here.

Access 57
KĒ IKI ROAD

Access 57 is a right turn onto Kē Iki Road, just after passing Sunset Beach Recreation Center on the left. The dirt path access is lush with vegetation on each side. There is a wood fence on the south side. The lava rock shelf on  the coastline at the north end of the right of way provides a great snorkeling site during the summer months. Boogie boarding and kayaking are also popular summer activities here. Big waves in the winter keep most people out of the water. To the north is "Cloud Break" surf site. No pubic amenities are available.

Access 58
KĒ IKI ROAD

Take the second right onto Kē Iki Road and follow to the left a few hundred feet. The paved road leads to the dirt pathway with a no parking sign and chain preventing cars from parking at the dead end. A stone wall with concrete stairway leads down to the beach. The fifty-foot-wide white sandy beach hosts gentle waves in the summer but becomes dangerous when the winter surf hits. The west end of the beach is bordered by Kulalua Point while a sweeping view lies to the east. Rocky shelves are scattered along the sandy shore with palm trees and naupaka bushes providing an upper border next to beach houses. Some surfing is doable during the summer months, but high waves make entry too dangerous in the winter.

Access 59
KĒ IKI ROAD

Turn right off Kamehameha Highway onto Kē Iki Road right before Shark's Cove. Parking is available along Kē Iki Road next to a bike path. The access is west on Kē Iki Road about twenty-five feet, clearly marked with a PROW sign and 276A emergency access sign. Proceed down the asphalt road that looks like a private driveway. Walk through the clearing in bushes to about 200 feet of rock to ocean. This area is known as Kulalua Point. The rock looks like solidified 'a'a lava. There are underwater caves here and small blowholes. Diving and snorkeling off the coast will delight all. The "Elevator Shaft," a popular

scuba dive entry point is located along the rocks. During the winter, the sea becomes tumultuous and dangerous. Huge waves crash up, and entry to the ocean is impossible.

Pūpūkea Beach Park and Uppers Surfing Support Park
59-727 KAMEHAMEHA HIGHWAY

This beach park encompasses the area between "Shark's Cove" to the north and "Three Tables" to the south. Shark's Cove has been rated as one of the "Top Twelve Shore Dives in the World." The entire area from Kulalua Point (the northern tip of Shark's Cove) to the Wānanapaoa Islets at the south end of Waimea Bay is a Marine Life Conservation District. Strict rules apply to fishing, and taking of marine life from these areas is prohibited. The area is a wonderland of impressive sea life for snorkelers and scuba divers to enjoy during the calmer summer months. Plenty of underwater caves and ledges can be explored near the north end of Shark's Cove including an entry point known as the Elevator Shaft, where divers descend fifteen feet down through a hole in the reef. The center area of the cove is great for snorkelers to observe a wide variety of fish hiding among the huge boulders scattered on the sandy bottom. Although there is no sandy beach here, the sparkling waters in the near shore tide pools provide entertainment for the small children and non-swimmers. Just to the south, past the fire station is Uppers Surfing Support Park. The area is better known as Three Tables, so named for the rock formations exposed in the center of the bay at low tide. This is a snorkeling area near shore, with diving opportunities a little further out to sea during the summer months. When the waves come up, it is a popular body-boarding site and surf site just off shore. There are no facilities here, but a short walk back near the fire station there are showers and restrooms.

Waimea Bay Beach Park
61-031 KAMEHAMEHA HIGHWAY

This picturesque bay is nestled at the end of Waimea Valley with a wide white sand beach that reaches around the mouth of the Waimea River. The name Waimea means "reddish water" and takes its name from the river that drains muddy water into the bay after heavy rains. The beach erodes during the winter months but the sand is redeposited in the summer. Activities vary with the time of year and surf conditions. When the bay is flat in the summer, it is perfect for swimming and snorkeling. The white sandy bottom is so clear it resembles a swimming pool. Reefs at each end of the bay attract turtles and fish. At the south end of the beach is a massive lava rock formation that is a favorite jumping spot for the not so faint of heart. Only the most experienced surfers should be near the water when waves come up in the winter; a dangerous shore break here has been responsible for numerous injuries and rescues. During the winter, waves can exceed twenty-five to thirty feet in this bay. The world's most elite big wave surfers await the call for the Quicksilver surf contest in Memory of Eddie Aikau to take place. Waves must pass the twenty-five-foot level for the contest to take place. The surf contest is so named to honor Eddie Aikau, the first lifeguard stationed at Waimea Bay who tragically lost his life at sea while attempting to rescue the *Hōkūleʻa*, when she capsized off Lānaʻi. Facilities include restrooms, showers, phones, some picnic tables in a grassy area under palm trees, and year round lifeguards on duty.

Leftovers Beach Access Park

This roadside undeveloped park is a simple stretch of beach. Several surf sites are accessible here such as "Leftovers" and "Alligators." There are patches of sandy beach at each end of the bay and some rocky tide pools to explore. Snorkeling and swimming are popular in the summer. There are no public facilities; the closest are at Waimea Bay Beach Park.

Kawailoa Beach Park
61-479 KAMEHAMEHA HIGHWAY

Kawailoa Beach Park, an undeveloped beach area, is a parcel owned by the City and County of Honolulu and named for the Kawailoa Stream, which empties into the ocean here. Parking is located across the street on the shoulder. The rocky shoreline and rip currents make this area unsuitable for swimming.

Chun's Reef Beach Support Park
61-529 KAMEHAMEHA HIGHWAY

About three miles past Haleʻiwa on Kamehameha Highway is an undeveloped beach park accessible by parking on the side of the road. This wide sandy beach leading to a shallow reef is named after local resident John Chun. Lava rock boulders dot the shore. This summer snorkeling and swimming spot transforms when winter waves create a favored surf site. In addition to the "Chun's Reef," "Jocko's" and "Piddley's" surf sites are also accessed here.

Laniākea Beach

This undeveloped beach park is easily found on Kamehameha Highway near Pōhaku Loa Way. About 1.5 miles out of Haleʻiwa town, all the cars and tour vans parked on the side of the road mark the beach. It is also known as Lani's

and Turtle Beach. Green sea turtles are frequently spotted feeding or basking in the sun due to seaweed-covered reefs next to shore. Green sea turtles are an endangered species so touching or handling them is against the law. A volunteer often sits at the beach to provide information and protect the turtles from curious by-standers. Snorkeling and swimming are great activities in calm summer months. During the winter when the waves kick up there are a number of surf sites located just off shore.

Access 60
61-785 PĀPAʻILOA ROAD
(NOT ON CITY AND COUNTY LIST)

From Kamehameha Highway one mile north of Haleʻiwa, turn left on Pāpaiʻiloa Road. Approximately .3 miles from the highway the access is on your right, well marked with the 269A emergency access sign and a PROW sign. Follow the shady dirt path through the palm trees to another hidden treasure found through the help of a renowned local surfer. This access has a panoramic view of Waimea Bay on the right all the way to Kaʻena Point on the left. Posh oceanfront homes nestle the shoreline with ironwood and palms providing shady spots

for picnicking. There is a reef located about one hundred feet to the right that provides wonderful snorkeling, fishing (pāpipi), and turtle watching opportunities. Turtles abound here as there is plenty of limu for them to feed on and they like to pull them-selves up on the beach for afternoon naps. Shallow pools are perfect for keiki, and during the summer the

calm waters invite swimmers and snorkelers to view the fish, turtles, and reefs near shore. The sandy shores extend forty feet for sunbathing.

Hale'iwa Beach Park
62-449 KAMEHAMEHA HIGHWAY

Low concrete seawalls that make it a perfect spot to watch people, boats, and sunsets line this quaint beach park located at the north end of Hale'iwa town. A couple of pergolas beckon you to set up your beach chairs and barbeque and stay for the day. With ample grassy area for athletic activities along with two basketball courts and two volleyball courts, children's playground and many ocean activities nearby, this spot is ideal for social gatherings. Facilities include picnic tables, showers, bathrooms, and phones. Canoe regatta races take place here at certain times of the year.

Ocean activities include jet skiing, stand up paddle boarding, scuba diving, snorkeling, canoeing, kayaking, and surfing. Rental facilities are located nearby. The narrow beach of a unique brown colored sand leads to a rocky shallow ocean bottom, which is not ideal for swimming. The "Hale'iwa Trench" scuba diving site is located offshore. The water is shallow, and a bit of a surface swim to get to the trench. This dive is located about 150 feet out in the boat channel so caution is urged. Turtles frequent the area and are additional wildlife eye candy for the diver. "Paean Point" surf spot is located just off shore.

Hale'iwa Ali'i Beach Park
66-167 HALE'IWA ROAD

Just to the west of the Hale'iwa Boat Harbor is Hale'iwa Ali'i Beach Park. The Kapahulu River splits the park into two sections. The eastern section of the park is a great fishing spot and access to the boat ramps at Hale'iwa Harbor. The western section is larger and expansive grassy areas lead up to the beach. The building may look familiar, as this was the primary set for *Baywatch Hawai'i*. Weekend festivals take place here at various times of the year. Facilities include showers, restrooms, and picnic areas. This beach is life guarded year round. A reef fronting the beach at the south end provides protection for swimmers. It is also a good spot for beginner surfers when the waves aren't too big. Stand up paddle boarding has become a popular activity here. In the winter, only experienced surfers should enter the waters here due to strong rip currents. This park is host to the Women's Triple Crown of Surfing events and the Hawaiian Reef Pro event. Top female surfers compete for a spot with the Association of Surfing Professionals. This is an alternate entry site to the Hale'iwa Trench dive spot.

North Shore History

The early Hawaiians were known to have settled here along the shores of the Anahulu River. In the mid-1800s, the western land system of ownership replaced the kahuna land system during the "Great Māhele." In 1848, a land redistribution act proposed by King Kamehameha III was enacted; it effectively paved the way for private land ownership. The land reverted from the king to private owners. About the same time, the first Western missionaries settled in Waialua Bay. They established the Queen Lili'uokalani Protestant Church, which still stands today. The surrounding lands quickly became cultivated fields of sugar cane and pineapple plantations that lasted for nearly a century.

In the late 1800s, an enterprising businessman named Benjamin Dillingham came to the area and helped shape its future. In 1865 Dillingham got a job as a clerk in a mercantile store supplying hardware to O'ahu's sugar industry. By 1869, he had purchased the store and expanded his business interests to agriculture when he saw the burgeoning potential of the sugar industry. He started to lease land in 'Ewa and Kahuku, but recognized the obstacle of getting the sugar to Honolulu. Ever the entrepreneur, he petitioned the King for a charter to build a railway and opened the first nine miles of his railway in 1889. In addition to transporting sugar and pineapple he could transport workers and businessmen to and from his plantations via the railroad and entice them to stay at his grand hotel. At its heyday, the O.R. & L railway extended 160 miles, from Honolulu Harbor to Kahuku Plantation. Dillingham is credited with naming Hale'iwa, because that was the name he bestowed on an elegant Victorian hotel he built at the base of the Anahulu River where it meets the ocean. He built the hotel to complement his other business ventures including the Waialua Sugar Company and the O.R. & L. Railway. The 1900s saw the waning of the great sugar plantations but savvy entrepreneurs took advantage of the opportunity to establish businesses to serve the plantation workers and tourists.

During the war years, the military played a heavy influence in Hale'iwa. The Air Corp built an airstrip near Hale'iwa Beach Park and took over the hotel as officer's quarters. Two airmen, George Welch and Kenneth Taylor, who were stationed there when the Japanese attacked Pearl Harbor, were credited with shooting down six Japanese planes as they attacked Pearl Harbor. Their heroic efforts were depicted in the movie *Tora, Tora, Tora*.

After the war and a 1946 tsunami that ripped up parts of the railroad, Hale'iwa slipped back to its sleepy plantation past. When Hawai'i achieved statehood and air transport started delivering tourists to O'ahu's shores, Hale'iwa began to prosper again and has fortunately maintained its charm and architectural heritage. Hale'iwa town with its quaint shops and art galleries along main street is the commercial center for the North Shore.

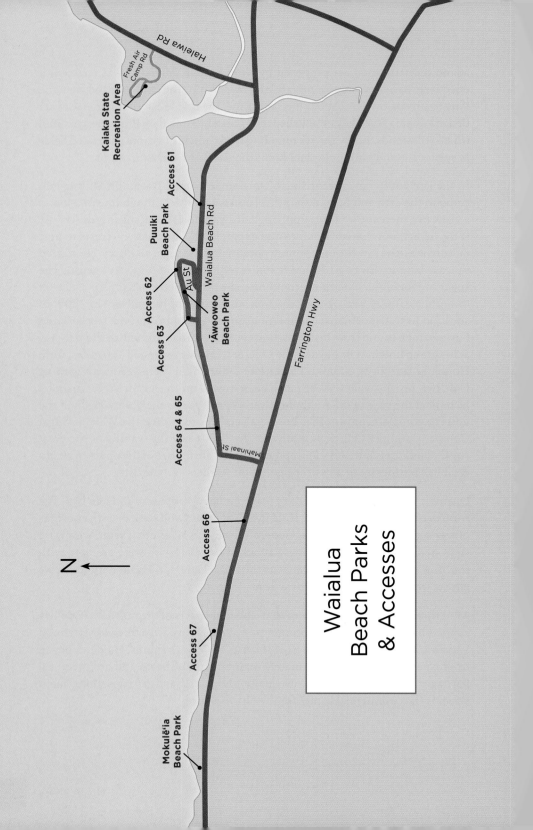

Waialua
Beach Parks
& Accesses

N

Haleiwa Rd

Fresh Air Camp Rd

Kaiaka State Recreation Area

Access 61

Puuiki Beach Park

Waialua Beach Rd

Access 62

Au St

Access 63

'Āweoweo Beach Park

Farrington Hwy

Access 64 & 65

Mahinaai St

Access 66

Access 67

Mokulē'ia Beach Park

WAIALUA
Beach Parks and Accesses 61 to 67

Waialua is located on the northwestern edge of Oʻahu. There are a few versions of how Waialua was so named. One story says that Waia, a ruthless aliʻi or chief ruled this area. He was known to have a corrupt government and he disregarded the priests and shunned religion. The people of the area suffered under his reign so they named the area after him. They combined Waia with lua which means two or double. Lua may refer to the two rivers that flow into Kaiaka Bay. Thus the meaning of Waialua is "doubly disgraced." There are three parks, Kaiaka Bay State Recreation is the most developed with camping available as well as restrooms, showers and picnic tables. ʻĀweoweo Beach Park has superior facilities to Mokulēʻia Beach Park with restrooms, showers, a playground, picnic tables, a basketball court and a sandy beach perfect for swimming. Of the eight accesses, it was access 66 that truly sparkled and we give it our five star rating. From the horses, to the polo fields and azure seas beyond, this access is perfect for swimming, snorkeling and sunbathing. Combine this access with a bike trip for an incomparable day in paradise.

To get to Waialua from Waikīkī, take Kalākaua Boulevard. east to Kapahulu Avenue and turn left. Continue on Kapahulu under the freeway and veer left on to Waiʻalae Avenue and the entrance to H1 west. Follow the H1 freeway through town, just past Pearl City take the H2 and head north. After passing Schofield Barracks on the left side of the road you will come to a "Y" intersection with signs directing you to Haleʻiwa or Waialua. Continue straight ahead on the main road to Waialua, when you reach a roundabout stay towards the left on Farrington Highway. You will reach the furthest and most scenic accesses from this road. To reach the easternmost accesses you will need to turn right onto Mahinaai Street and then another right onto Crozier Drive.

For bus riders from Honolulu, use the 52 Wahiawā-Circle Island route. Accesses 64 to 67 are not available via the bus.

The bike path starts at the intersection of Kamehameha Highway and Waialua Beach Road. It is a wide asphalt path that runs parallel to Waialua Beach Road and terminates at Crozier Drive. Travel west on Crozier Drive until the road ends at Mahinaai Street, turn left and follow this road until it meets Farrington Highway. Turn right, follow Farrington Highway until it dead-ends at a dirt

parking lot in Kaʻena Point State Recreation Area, only four-wheel drive can continue on the heavily rutted dirt road. The scenery is unparalleled as you pass Dillingham Airfield with the colorful parachutes of skydivers dotting the skies above. The mountain vistas on one side of the road and sapphire seas on the other are awe inspiring.

Kaiaka State Recreation Area
66-449 HALEʻIWA ROAD

Located off of Haleʻiwa Road this large fifty-three-acre park is set at the northern tip of Kaiaka Bay where the Kiʻikiʻi and Paukauila Streams empty into the bay. Kaiaka meaning "shadowy sea" is appropriately named as the bay appears brown at times from the soil runoff deposited by the two streams. This is a popular fishing area and there are seven camping sites available to the public with permits issued by the Department of Land and Natural Resources. Swimmers will find the northernmost beaches the best for swimming and there is access to a few surf spots such as "Hammerheads" just off shore. Beware if you are surfing here, it's named Hammerheads for a reason as this is a shark breeding ground. Parking, restrooms, showers, and picnic tables are among the facilities provided here.

Access 61
WAIALUA BEACH ROAD

Located next to Kauihi Stream Bridge on Waialua Beach Road, there is parking for a few cars on a dirt patch in front of the access. There is a bus stop directly across Waialua Beach Road where you can exit from the 76 Waialua Shuttle. It is a wide access about forty feet across with houses on one side and a trickling stream on the right side. The beach was strewn with debris, wood, and shells probably from the stream dumping into the ocean after rains. Westward the beach is about forty to fifty feet wide in front of the seaside homes. Eastward there are some interesting palm tree shacks fronting the homes where they may provide shelter for boats. You can follow the beach quite a ways. The water was churned up, brown and uninviting, effects of Kauihi Stream flowing down onto the shoreline from Wahiawā's Lake Wilson. A local informed us this is a periodic occurrence and during dry times the water is clearer and more inviting.

Puʻuiki Beach Park
WAIALUA BEACH ROAD BETWEEN KAIEA PLACE AND APUHIHI STREET

Located just west of Kaiaka Bay on Waialua Beach Road this small private beach park has no facilities. Although it is currently not part of the park system maintained by the City and County of Honolulu, there is a proposal to buy this parcel to add to the park system. This beach was originally owned by the Waialua Sugar Company and maintained for the benefit of their employees. The beach is narrow at this point but the shallow reef provides snorkeling and spear fishing opportunities. Surf spots can also be accessed outside the reef.

Access 62
AʻU STREET A

To reach this access take Waialua Beach Road turn left on Apuhihi Street towards the ocean, the road ends at Aʻu Street. The access is located to the west of a five story apartment complex on Aʻu Street. Follow the path along the complex and you will come out on more beach-fronting apartments and houses on both sides. The beach is under water at high tide in front of the apartments to the west. There is a debris strewn beach to the east, turtles frequent the area and feed near the shore line on the seaweed covered reef.

ʻĀweoweo Beach Park
68-197 AʻU STREET

This tiny beach park is located between accesses 62 and 63 on Aʻu Street. The park is a quaint neighborhood park complete with swing sets, basketball courts, picnic tables, showers and restrooms. Although there is not much shade to be had here the beach is exemplary for tanning and the shallow sandy bottom of the ocean is perfect for swimming.

Access 63
A'U STREET B

From Waialua Beach Road turn makai (towards the ocean) on 'Āweoweo Street. When the road turns into A'u Street you have reached the access. If traveling by bus, transfer from the 52 Circle Island bus to the 76 Waialua Shuttle. The bus travels the length of Akule Street which is parallel to A'u Street so you can reach access 62 and 63 by exiting at either end of Akule Street. The access is located between two homes, on the west side is a rock pillar with a pineapple on top. This access looks like you are walking through the homeowners yard as the property line is not clearly marked. The beach is about ten to fifteen feet wide at high tide. There is a reef and sandy bottom, but the water looks churned up here.

Access 64 and 65
CROZIER BROW PARKING

From Farrington Highway turn north onto Mahinaai Street and then right onto Crozier Drive. This access has its own parking area located off the narrow lane. A tree-lined shady path between two chain-link fences comes out in the middle of a neighborhood of houses fronting the ocean. The ocean is cleaner here. Plenty of beach to walk along with lovely sandy-bottom patches to swim in. The reef extends out quite a ways so you can swim or snorkel, just don't go out too far due to cross currents. If you walk to the west you can connect to access 66 about one mile down the shore. There is a surf site located to the left of the access called "Silva's Channel."

We couldn't find a second access after numerous attempts of driving up and down Crozier Drive. Possibly the ample parking lot is considered another public access in itself, as the accesses are listed and located at the city and county's discretion.

Access 66
Makaleha Beach Park
68-539 FARRINGTON HIGHWAY

This five star access is easily missed. While traveling west on Farrington Highway look for a field of palm trees with a gate and sign for Dillingham Lodge on your left. The access is located about fifty feet past the gate on the right hand side of the road. There is ample parking on both sides of the highway. Be sure not to leave any valuables behind because in this isolated area break-ins to your car could occur. It is located about two miles south of access 67 and the beach can be followed from one access to the next at low tide.

Follow the shady path alongside the horse paddock toward the ocean. The path opens up to a wide sandy beach. This area is sometimes referred to as Makaleha Beach Park, although there are no amenities available here. The name Makaleha which means "to look about in wonder or admiration" comes from the stream that empties nearby. There is plenty here for families with small children to see and do. Well tended and handsome horses grazed the fields we walked through.

The ocean is shallow and there are plenty of coral reefs and sandy patches to swim or snorkel in. This is a perfect place for a lazy day spent lounging in the shade of ironwood trees. Dillingham Airfield is nearby and delivers frequent entertainment by way of parachuters and hang glider planes drifting down to the airfield. The beach extends in both directions unobstructed by rocks. To the east, the beach fronts the paddocks. You can walk along close to the fence until you reach some bushes and trees. If you follow a small path between the bushes and the fence you will come across about ten small clearings nestled in the foliage that provide shelter from the sun and wind. This area is known as a nude beach and signs are posted warning of fines for nude sunbathing but it hasn't deterred some people.

Monk seals, an endangered species, are occasional visitors to these shores as illustrated by signs warning people to not disturb them. Recently an Alaskan tourist made a film harassing a seal and posted it on YouTube. He subsequently was arrested and charged with a felony.

To the west, the beach fronts the Mokulēʻia Polo Fields. The Hawaiʻi Polo Club holds matches at this polo field on many Sundays during its half year polo season which begins in May. 2010 marked the 45th year of this club that has almost 140 years of polo history in Hawaiʻi. Visiting polo teams come from as far away as Argentina and England. The club dubs its matches "Polo by the Sea" and hosts unique games where the backdrop is rolling surf and white sandy beaches. The polo matches are open to the public. There is an $8 entry fee. Games start at 2 PM and food and drinks can be purchased.

Access 67
Hoʻomana Beach

This westernmost access is reached by turning right on Hoʻomana Place from Farrington Highway. Street parking is on a quiet cul-de-sac about halfway down on the left. The beach is about twenty feet wide at low tide. At high tide, the beach is swallowed up to the seawalls fronting the houses. To the west, the beach is narrow and gets washed up. To the east you can walk to a dried up stream outlet. Continuing .25 miles eastward, the beach gives way to a long seawall in front of the Mokulēʻia Beach Colony. Even at low tide we watched the waves wash right up to the rock wall. Stairs provide entry to the top of the rock wall, where signs proclaim that public access is allowed. After crossing some large boulders and another shorter rock wall the beach begins again directly in front of the Mokulēʻia Polo Fields.

Activities include swimming and snorkeling as the ocean is a combination of shallow reef and sandy pockets. The reef extends out quite a ways so it is protected from the big breakers. Be cautious before entering the ocean as there can be dangerous cross currents even in the summer. In winter the entire North Shore is known for its large and unpredictable waves. Heed all the warning signs you see at the seawall. There are seven of them and they are there for a good reason.

Mokulēʻia Beach Park
68-919 KAʻENA POINT ROAD

This 38.5-acre park takes its name from the large land division in Waialua. The name Mokulēʻia means "district of abundance." The beach park with its shallow reef and sandy shore has been heavily used and shows the signs of wear. The public restrooms have been replaced by a few Porta Potties, although there is still running water. A few battered picnic tables remain. Since it is the last beach park on this end of the island it is frequented by all types of different users from the traditional fisherman to the kite and wind surfers who find challenging conditions during kona or southerly winds. Snorkeling, diving, and spearfishing are popular activities during calm seas in the summer months. Surfers have access to a couple of sites off shore with especially large waves in the winter.

Waialua History

Hawaiians settled in the Waialua area around 1100 AD and built villages along valleys, streams, and bays. These fertile lands were sprinkled with natural springs allowing abundant growth of taro and sweet potato.

Sugar became Hawai'i's major industry in the late nineteenth century and much of O'ahu's land was divided into sugar plantations. Native Hawaiians were the first cane field workers. As labor needs grew, plantation owners recruited immigrants from China, Portugal, Japan, and the Philippines to work in their fields and mills. When the immigrants arrived in O'ahu, they were sent to different plantations; one of these was at Waialua.

Like 'Ewa Beach and Wai'anae, the town of Wailalua's more recent history revolves around its sugar mill. In 1898, Castle & Cooke formed the Waialua Agricultural Company and purchased a small plantation from the Halstead Brothers. Castle & Cooke built a new mill, expanded the acreage, built a small railway system, and maximized water storage giving the Waialua sugar plantation the largest water storage capacity in Hawai'i. Sugar production increased fourfold from 1900 to 1905.

Around this time visionary businessman Benjiman Franklin Dillingham was the director of Waialua Sugar Company. Dillingham's new railroad joined Waialua's sugar plantation to Wai'anae's and 'Ewa Beach's sugar plantation and on to Honolulu Harbor. Eventually his rail would run all the way to the sugar mill in Kahuku. Dillingham had his fingers in many pies, including Dole Food Company, a hardware store, Dillingham Dairy Ranch, and the Hale'iwa

Hotel, which was conveniently located along his railroad. Today, in Waialua the Dillingham Ranch with its adjacent airfield and polo field are still in use. Dillingham Ranch no longer produces dairy, but is now an equestrian center that offers horseback tours. Dillingham and his son were ardent polo fans and though they sold the field in the 1960s it is still in use. Dillingham Airfield was built in 1927 with a 5,000 by seventy-five-foot runway. It went through several Hawaiian names, but after the attack on Pearl Harbor, it was pressed into military service as Dillingham Airfield. In 1948, the airfield was shut down. Decades later the airfield was reactivated for civilian use by the military. The airfield is home to recreational aircraft and activities with occasional military use. Tour companies providing parachuting, glider rides and ultralight aircraft rides are located here providing a steady stream of airborne entertainment while laying on the beach. By 1991, Waialua Sugar Company, as part of the Dole Food Company, was producing eight percent of the sugar in Hawai'i. Over time the plantation was unable to increase its yield and the Waialua Sugar Mill closed in October 1996 due to poor profits. It was the last sugar plantation on the island of O'ahu.

If you are a fan of the TV show *Lost* you will be interested to know that the plane crash scene was filmed at the western end of Mokulē'ia. Several episodes were also filmed at Dillingham Ranch.

You can still see the stack of the sugar mill in the unique and picturesque town of Waialua. The mill itself and the railroads are gone, but this quaint village with its airfield, polo field, and equestrian center still thrives. In recent times, Waialua residents have been strong opponents to developers promoting golf gateway communities like those seen in 'Ewa Beach. We wonder how long Waialua will be able to maintain its rural charm.

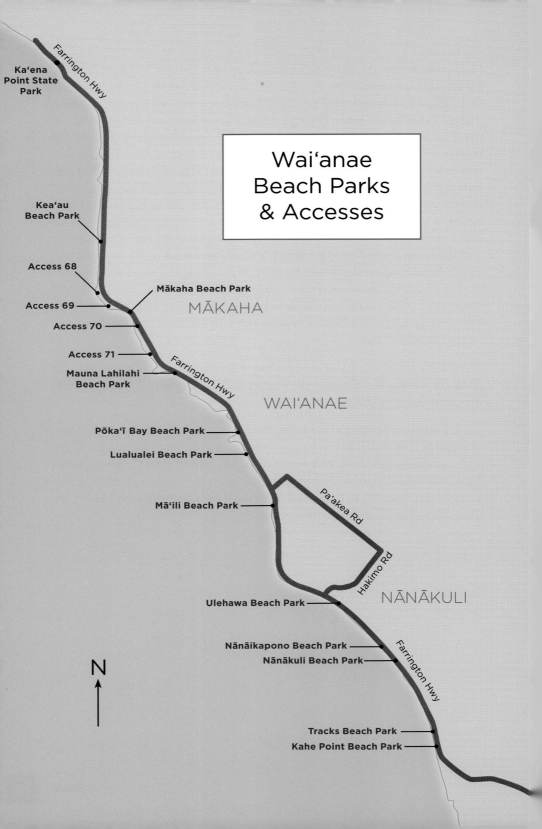

Wai'anae
Beach Parks
& Accesses

Ka'ena Point State Park

Farrington Hwy

Kea'au Beach Park

Access 68

Access 69

Access 70

Mākaha Beach Park

MĀKAHA

Access 71

Mauna Lahilahi Beach Park

Farrington Hwy

WAI'ANAE

Pōka'ī Bay Beach Park

Lualualei Beach Park

Mā'ili Beach Park

Pa'akea Rd

Hakimo Rd

Ulehawa Beach Park

NĀNĀKULI

Nānāikapono Beach Park

Nānākuli Beach Park

Farrington Hwy

Tracks Beach Park

Kahe Point Beach Park

N

WAIʻANAE
Beach Parks and Accesses 68 to 71

Waiʻanae means "waters of the ʻanae or mullet fish." The ancient Hawaiians probably found plenty of mullet off of Oʻahu's northwestern shores. This Leeward Side of Oʻahu has a spectacular coastline speckled with beach parks hugging Farrington Highway. Jeremy Harris, who was Honolulu mayor from 1994 to 2004, envisioned a lei of public parks around the island. Harris' strong influence pushed the prolific park presence you see in Waiʻanae today. The sapphire sea is a pristine panorama out your driver's window as you cruise along. For ease of navigating purposes, we have reversed directions for this section starting closest to Waikīkī and ending at the northwestern tip of the island where the road dead-ends. The beach parks begin just after turning north, past Ko ʻOlina. The four rights of way fall between Mauna Lahilahi Beach Park and Keaʻau Beach Park. Mākaha Beach Park is amid these accesses. In recent years the homeless population was forced from Honolulu and Waikīkī and some of them moved to Waiʻanae beaches and parks. The Keaulanas, a renowned local surfing family, keeps Mākaha Beach Park free of the homeless, making it the safest haven in wild western Oʻahu. To get there, take H1 west, eventually H1 becomes Farrington Highway. All of the parks and accesses are located along this road. From Honolulu, take the 40 bus or in the afternoon, take 93 Waiʻanae Coast Express bus. Biking is not safe on Farrington Highway, since narrow or nonexistent bike lanes and speedy traffic make accidents likely.

Kahe Point Beach Park
92-301 FARRINGTON
HIGHWAY

Just a mile past the Ko ʻOlina turnoff is the first of many beach parks. Ragged jade mountains descend into a deep blue ocean for a stunning western vista. Kahe Point located across from Hawaiian Electric's Kahe Power Plant is known for its superior snorkeling and diving activities. You will probably

see commercial dive or snorkeling boats docked off shore in calm seas. Two pipes release warm water from the electric plant here, which attracts all kinds of tropical fish, turtles, and even spinner dolphins. Sharks are also known to frequent these waters, so frequently scan your surrounding waters and be cautious. A small sand beach strewn with rocks makes an easy entry when the ocean is calm. When the waves are up there is a small surf break south of here. Shaded picnic pavilions and rundown restrooms and showers are functional. Stow your valuables as this area is known for car break-ins.

Tracks Beach Park
92-271 FARRINGTON HIGHWAY

Just after Kahe Power Plant on the left side of the highway, is an unmarked entrance to this park. It was established with funds set aside by Hawaiian Electric for reestablishment of the surf site they inadvertently destroyed when they were extending the cooling water outfall into deeper water. This largely undeveloped fourteen-acre park has only a bathroom, shower area and a small grassy area with a picnic table. When surf is up locals flock here, despite the rocky entry. When calmer waters prevail snorkeling becomes a pleasant activity.

Nānākuli Beach Park
86-269 FARRINGTON HIGHWAY

Nānākuli means "to look at the knee." This forty-acre beach park is every community's fantasy; complete with baseball fields and basketball courts on the north end and beautiful sandy shores on the south end. The beach entry to the ocean is gentle and perfect for swimming during the summer months. Check with the lifeguards in the winter for strong currents and high surf. With coral reefs off shore, there is excellent snorkeling and scuba diving when seas are calm. There are also restrooms, showers, picnic tables, phones, and a large parking lot available.

Nānāikapono Beach Park

Nānāikapono means "to look to the righteous." Located just across the road from the Pacific Shopping Mall, this small beach park offers parking, restrooms, and showers.

Ulehawa Beach Park
87-1581 FARRINGTON HIGHWAY

The literal translation of Ulehawa is "dirty penis" and likely the name of a chief who lived here. This mile long, largely undeveloped fifty-eight-acre park is broken up by a community of houses.
Once a popular place for the homeless, the park has recently undergone renovation. Bodysurfers, snorkelers, and swimmers are known to frequent a shallow lagoon that fronts the park. Fishing is another preferred activity here. Restrooms, showers, and picnic tables are available. The park starts at Princess Kahanu Road and extends to Maipalaoa Road where .25 miles of houses are located; the park then continues to Māʻili stream outlet.

Māʻili Beach Park
87-021 FARRINGTON HIGHWAY

This long stretch of grass field leading up to a wide strand of white sand beach is known for surfing and outrigger canoe races. The shore is made up of pebbly white rocks or "ʻili" for which the park takes its name. The surf breaks all year at this beach but access can be tricky over the coral. There are three surf breaks in the area, "Māʻili Point" to the south, "Tumble Land" accessed from Ule-

hawa Beach Park, and "Māʻili Rights" accessed from Māʻili Beach Park. All areas are for the intermediate to expert surfer. Sharks are known to frequent this area. The beach is widest during the summer months but erodes away during the winter. Swimming is possible in the calm summer months, but care should be taken because of the offshore coral reefs. Most weekends the grassy area of the park is crowded by tents and bouncy houses for a myriad of local celebrations. Permits are available through the city and county offices to reserve a site. Lifeguards are on duty year round, there are bathrooms, showers, parking, phones, picnic tables, and barbeque grills.

Lualualei Beach Park
86-113 FARRINGTON HIGHWAY

One Hawaiian meaning of lualualei is "flexible reef." In the battle of Kīpapa of 1410 AD Waiʻanae chiefs sent their warriors to encircle invaders like a reef. This eighteen-acre park across the street from the Waiʻanae Sewage Treatment Plant, begins at Māʻiliʻili Channel and extends to Lualualei Homestead Road. The rocky shore makes it unsafe for swimming but there is a surf site just off shore known as "Sewers." Fishing is also a popular activity here. The undeveloped part of the beach park area extends along Pōkaʻī Bay Drive. The stench from the sewage treatment plant when the winds are blowing may limit your time. Restrooms, showers, and a parking lot are available.

Pōkaʻī Bay Beach Park
85-037 WAIʻANAE VALLEY ROAD

This fifteen-acre beach park is reached by turning left at Waiʻanae Valley Road and following until you drive straight into the parking lot. The beach was named after a Hawaiian chief named Pōkaʻī whose name means "Night of the Supreme One." This is a great spot for families with small children or those who prefer no wave action. It is a quiet cove where beachgoers can enjoy powdery white sand from beach to ocean. Outrigger canoes, small boats, and stand up paddle boarders go in and out of the bay. Fishing is excellent just off the breakwater that protects the cove. Beginning surfers can give the small waves that form off a reef in the center of the bay a try or move further north to some breaks in front of the Army Rest Camp. To the left is Kanelilo Point where an ancient fishing "heiau" or temple is located. There are restrooms, showers, picnic tables under big shade trees, barbeque grills, and lifeguards on duty. A Farmer's Market is held here every Friday between 11:00 and 11:45 AM.

Mauna Lahilahi Beach Park
84-1161 FARRINGTON HIGHWAY

This nine-acre park is hidden off Farrington Highway on Lahilahi Street. Look for a tall slender mountain and find the park at its base. "Lahilahi" means "thin" and "mauna" means "mountain." The beach is narrow and attempts by the city to reestablish the sandy shore have been made. Parking, restrooms, and showers are available. Preferred activities are swimming, surfing, and fishing.

Access 71
MOUA STREET

This access provides a breathtaking view of Turtle Beach against the backdrop of Mauna Lahilahi. At high tide the beach is nonexistent and one must stand precariously atop a cement wall to look out. Barking dogs in chain linked yards on both sides of this right of way are unnerving. At low tide you can walk on the western reef to a sandy cove where you can enter the water. To the left you is a sharp coral reef, that can be stepped over to get down to the beach. Use caution if you choose to walk the reefs as rouge waves can catch one unaware even at low tide.

Access 70
'UPENA STREET

From Farrington Highway take the second 'Upena Street on the left; the access is five houses down on the right. Located between two chain-link fences on a dusty lane, this PROW leads to a narrow beach about twenty feet wide then a large drop-off to the rocky ocean. The landscape of this right of way changes throughout the year. During the  winter, this beach changes to a sandy shore access because the sand shifts from Mākaha Beach (about .25 miles to the west) to this end. You can reach Mākaha Beach throughout the year by walking close to the rock walls abreast of the oceanfront homes. It is a short walk to Mākaha Beach where there is a safe entry for snorkeling, diving, surfing, and boogie boarding.

Eastward is a rocky outcropping; keep close to the rock walls of the oceanfront homes. This walk is unsuitable for the elderly or small children as the rocks are very sharp and you will be occasionally sprayed by big waves. There are many tide pools to look at as you walk. During the summer this is a nice place to fish.

 This walk is not recommended during the winter months as the waves can be up to ten feet and could wash one out to sea. Use caution throughout the year, as even in summer the surf could be up. Parking is on the side of 'Upena Street and it is .6 miles to the nearest bathroom and shower facility at Mākaha Beach Park.

Mākaha Beach Park
84-369 FARRINGTON HIGHWAY

"Mākaha" or "fierce" beach is famous worldwide for its surfing waves. During the winter season, waves up to twenty-five feet high break off Mākaha Point, providing some of the most challenging big waves in Hawai'i. There are two surf breaks here worth exploring, the "Mākaha" break and "Klausmeyers" which is just south. The Buffalo's Big Board Surfing Classic is held here in February or March in honor of "Buffalo Keaulana" a local surfing legend who was a lifeguard at this beach for many years. He is retired now but his son Brian has carried on his work as lifeguard and they take pride in keeping the beach clean and safe. When the surf isn't pumping in, there are some spectacular snorkeling and diving spots located just off shore. There is a north reef nearer to Kepuhi Point that is accessible by the apartments, or use access 69 to avoid the swim out to the caverns. Just off "Kepuhi" or "blowhole" Point to the left is a statue that sits about thirty-five feet under water. No one knows why or how it landed there, but it makes for an interesting dive. There is a South Reef that is better suited for diving. It is located directly in front of the second lifeguard stand. You have to swim out about seventy feet to get to it. There are a couple of drop-off areas around the reef and two deep caves to explore.

Access 69
SOUTH END OF MAKAU STREET

Directly at the end of this right of way is a "kepuhi" or "blowhole," a hole at the inland end of a sea cave through which waves funnel up and out. Hence the name this area was given, Kepuhi Point. Several blow holes are between access 68 and access 69. There is ample parking on Makau Street. Mākaha Beach Park is .3 miles eastward on Farrington Highway.

Access 68
NORTH END OF MAKAU STREET

From Farrington Highway take a right onto Makau Street and follow it until right before it curves back toward the highway. The access is about two to three houses before the curve in the road. There is parking available on the roadside. Access is between two rock coral walls. If you walk .25 miles westward over the coral rock reef, you will be at Kea'au Beach Park. Making your way .25 miles eastward over the rocky shoreline, you will come to another access way that is unmarked for the public (intersection of Lawai'a Street and Makau Street) Climbing eastward over more large rocks you will come to the other or easternmost public access on Makau Street. This access is .3 miles from the first access. Although the two accesses can be reached by navigating the very rocky coral reef, one should be wary of large waves, and avoid doing this at high tide. This shore walk would not be wise for young children or the elderly. Entry to the water is not advised but there are plenty of places to cast a fishing rod and we saw locals doing so.

Kea'au Beach Park
83-431 FARRINGTON HIGHWAY

"Kea'au" or "rippling of the sea" has a rocky limestone shelf that fronts the park. There is no swimming here due to the sharp coral reef rock, but it's a great place to fish. We observed a half dozen local fishermen. Snorkelers, scuba divers, and surfers can enter the ocean at the west end of Kea'au Park, where a sandy beach begins along the shore. For divers the entry is at the north end of the park, and underwater features include lava tubes, canyons, an archway and a drop-off about 1,800 feet from shore. Tons of coral cover the coast. The city and county recently renovated the parks facilities and evicted the homeless, creating a pleasant picnic area with an azure panorama of ocean all the way to Ka'ena Point. Parking, restrooms, showers, and picnic tables are available here.

Ka'ena Point State Park
END OF THE ROAD ON FARRINGTON HIGHWAY

This jewel at the end of the road provides stunning views of jade mountains rolling down to turquoise sea. The white sand beaches are studded with occasional reef and tide pools that keep small ones entertained. The ocean is fickle here—sometimes calm and serene, and other times pounding the shoreline and anything that gets in its way. Surfing is only for the more experienced, and a check with the lifeguard on duty is advised. On a calm summer day snorkeling and diving are pleasant adventures with plenty of fish and turtles to see at the south end of the beach by a rocky outcropping known as Pukano Point. A word of warning: the beach entry can be deceiving because of a strong undertow. A fifteen- to twenty-minute study from the beach observing waves is advised. The beach is best known as "Yokohama" or "Yoks" named after a Japanese fisherman who frequented the area. Shore fishing is a favored activity at the north end of the beach all the way out to Ka'ena Point. A railroad at one time went around the island but has since fallen into disrepair. The road is only accessible part way with a four-wheel drive. A moderately easy hike out to the northwestern tip of the island is along the old dusty road. During the winter months, hikers will be treated to a view of nesting albatross near the point as

well as frolicking whales just off shore, and an occasional napping monk seal on the beach. Tide pools are explorable if you get to Ka'ena Point but swimming activities are not recommended due to the cross currents.

Wai'anae History

Before Kamehameha united the islands in 1795, a valley such as Mākaha was called an "ahupua'a" and would have been run by a manager known as a "konohiki." Sometimes a konohiki was a chief, but he always answered to a chief above him. While the chiefs had the power of life and death over commoners, they had two strong reasons for treating them fairly: tax collection and defense against other invading chiefs. The commoners were free to leave any area or chief and join another. Since the chiefs often waged war against each other, it was in their interest to keep their people happy. After Kamehameha the chiefs no longer competed for subjects, but competed for wealth.

In 1778, Captain Cook discovered what he called the "Sandwich Isles." He sighted Mauna Lahilahi before sailing on to Kaua'i and wrote about it in his log. In the early 1800s ships anchored along the Wai'anae Coast where there were large forests of sandalwood on the mountain slopes. The trees were cut down and shipped to China.

Chief Boki, the appointed governor of Oʻahu, and chief of the Waiʻanae District, pushed his subjects to harvest more of the sandalwood, neglecting the tending of crops and catching of fish. The wood was sold in China for a large profit. Trade goods included needles, nails, pins, scissors, clothing, kitchen utensils, and even ships. In 1829, when Boki found himself in debt, and the sandalwood trees gone, he went searching for a nearby island rich in sandalwood. He set sail with two ships and was never seen again.

Around this time Christian missionaries from the United States were baptizing and converting the Hawaiians. Although Boki was a baptized Christian, he refused to marry Liliha in a church. He was a skilled practitioner of Hawaiian medicine as taught by the kahuna.

Thus the Waiʻanae people's moral and religious lifestyles remained unchanged for many years. Man and woman lived together without benefit of marriage. People prayed to the Hawaiian gods and the kahuna practiced their ancient ways.

In the late 1840s, many Hawaiians became sick and started dying. Much of this was due to exposure to new diseases that the sailors and missionaries had brought, but the lack of crops and fish only made things worse. In 1835 a census listed 1,654 residents on the Waiʻanae coast. A series of epidemics began in 1848 including smallpox which in 1853 spread to the Waiʻanae Coast. Less than 800 people were left when it was finally stamped out in early 1854.

In 1855 Robert William Holt, a partner in the James Robinson firm, Hawaiʻi's first shipyard, acquired Mākaha Valley from High Chief Pākī for $5,000. Robert William Holt was part-Hawaiian and rich, a member of the aliʻi or nobility. Mākaha Valley became a ranch, when one of Holt's sons, Owen Jones Holt, decided to transform his acreage into a luxurious "country estate" where his mother and wife, who were both aliʻi, could live a royal Hawaiian life of leisure.

The Holt ranch included a large, two-story house on a knoll by a stream, guest and servant cottages designed for as many as one hundred guests, bath houses on the beach, with a pier so guests could visit without sandy feet. He loved horse racing and built stables and a race track. Gardens surrounded the house with all kinds of fruit and flowering trees. Holt kept a zoo with wild turkeys, gifts to him from visiting ship captains. Peacocks were a gift from Kamehameha V, who with his family were often guests. Holt hired the Hawaiians of Mākaha to herd his cattle and tend his taro patches and gardens. This made the Waiʻanae Hawaiians happy, but the population still declined.

In 1902 after the death of James Robinson Holt II, heir to the Holt Ranch, court battles began between the Holt siblings. Most of the Holt fortune went to attorneys and much of the rest was sold to the Wai'anae Sugar Plantation.

In 1876 Hermann A. Wideman took advantage of the fact that the United States Congress passed a treaty which allowed Hawaiian sugar to enter the U.S. duty free. He started the first sugar plantation on O'ahu in Wai'anae Valley. This created new jobs and suddenly the population grew.

Around this time, Benjamin Dillingham installed a railway that ran from Honolulu all the way to Wai'anae, and what had once been a day-long horse ride, was now a less than a two-hour train ride. The railway continued from Mākaha and Makua around Ka'ena Point to Mokulē'ia and by 1899 Dillingham's railroad had reached the sugar plant in Kahuku. In the 1940s Wai'anae's sugar industry collapsed due to more economically feasible foreign markets.

Chinn Ho was the grandson of a Chinese immigrant who arrived in 1875 to care for coconut trees. He was a self-made millionaire who followed two business philosophies: "Kill them with kindly competition" and "Achieve success by sharing your success with others." When he heard about the Wai'anae plantation's vote to shut down, he bought 9,150 acres for $1.25 million. This was the largest land buy by an Asian in Hawai'i. Over the next few years, Ho and his Capital Investment Group took in $4 million by subdividing lots and selling off 4,000 acres. Unlike other profit seekers, it was Chinn Ho's dream to provide affordable housing for anyone who wanted it. First Ho sold off the prime beach lots at $2,500 to generate cash. The other parcels he sold for as little as ten cents per square foot to former plantation workers. Seventy percent of the former workers bought their houses, and the population grew. In the 1960s Ho built the Mākaha Inn and several golf courses. Mākaha Shores, Mākaha Valley Towers, Mākaha Beach Cabanas, Mākaha Surfside, Mākaha Valley Plantation, and Hawaiian Princess Condominiums were built by other developers soon after. Chinn Ho died in 1987 and is buried in Mākaha Valley.

Wild western Wai'anae has been a last hold-out for many: Chief Boki allowed the kahuna's ways to continue long after the missionaries arrived. Holt provided Hawaiians with ways to make a living that were familiar to them. Chinn Ho provided affordable homes for sugar plantation workers, many who were Hawaiian. Though the City and County have cleared out most of the beach parks, today Wai'anae is the last hold out for many homeless living on its shores.

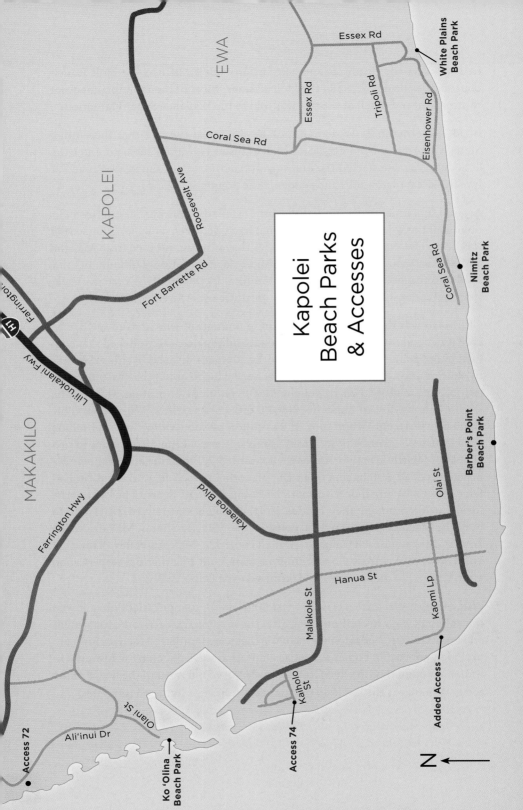

Kapolei
Beach Parks
& Accesses

'EWA

KAPOLEI

MAKAKILO

Essex Rd

Essex Rd

Essex Rd

Tripoli Rd

Eisenhower Rd

White Plains
Beach Park

Coral Sea Rd

Roosevelt Ave

Coral Sea Rd

Nimitz
Beach Park

Fort Barrette Rd

Farrington

H1

Lili'uokalani Fwy

Barber's Point
Beach Park

Farrington Hwy

Kalaeloa Blvd

Olai St

Hanua St

Kaomi Lp

Malakole St

Added Access

Kaiholo St

Access 74

Olani St

Ali'inui Dr

Ko 'Olina
Beach Park

Access 72

N

KAPOLEI
Beach Parks and Accesses 72 to 74

Puʻu o Kapolei is a volcanic cone on Oʻahu's leeward side. Puʻu means hill and Kapolei means beloved Kapo. According to legend, Kapo was sister to Pele, the fire goddess. Ancient Hawaiians used this landmark along with the sunset as a calender to mark their two seasons. Planned as Oʻahu's "second city," Kapolei takes its name from the volcanic cone. Kapolei, a young community being developed as an urban center, will be second in size only to Honolulu. Although the newest city on the island, the three beach accesses Kapolei contains have unique and older histories, one dating back to Queen Kaʻahumanu. Home to Ko ʻOlina Resort, Campbell Industrial Park, and a decommissioned naval air station (now Kalaeloa Community District), Kapolei is a curious collage of the young and ancient, luxurious and scrappy, militant and mundane.

To reach these accesses, drive west on H1. Take the Ko ʻOlina exit about two miles past the end of the freeway to reach accesses 72 and 73. For access 74, take Kalaeloa Road/Campbell Industrial Park exit 1. For the remaining beach parks take Kapolei/Makakilo exit 2. More specific directions are listed before each access.

Limited bus service to these accesses necessitates a long walk from your drop-off point. The Route 41 bus will take you from town to Kapolei Transit Center where you will transfer to the appropriate bus listed for each access.

The shady main thoroughfare through Ko ʻOlina is only five miles round trip providing well marked bike lanes minus heavy traffic. Get there early as the parking lots fill quickly and security guards turn cars away when lots are full. Another biking adventure in Kalaeloa connects Nimitz Beach to White Plains Beach along mostly deserted roads bordering the Coast Guard Station and the ocean.

Access 72
Paradise Cove
92-1101 ALIʻI-NUI STREET

This access is hidden between Lanikūhonua and Paradise Cove. After passing the Ko ʻOlina guard shack enter at the third driveway on the right. The parking

lot is on the right and open from sunrise to sunset with 13 parking spaces and two handicapped stalls. The nearest bathroom facility and shower is at lagoon one at Ko 'Olina resort. It is .3 miles away and located at the end of the fourth right turn after the guard shack.

From the parking lot follow the sidewalk west towards Paradise Cove parking lot.

Turn left at the sign and follow a tree-shaded dirt path towards the beach.

Secluded, when compared to the crowds at the four man-made lagoons to the east, turtles often swim in this remote cove. Its sandy bottom is protected by an outer ring of reef, creating a cozy niche to snorkel and swim. Local families frolic here, especially on the weekends. A beautiful white sandy beach about forty feet wide fronts this natural lagoon, perfect for children. Directly east of the lagoon is Lanikūhonua, a private area once owned by the former Campbell Estate, but now a part of a non-profit organization. There is no safe passage through Lanikūhonua to reach lagoon one at Ko 'Olina Resort. At the west end of the lagoon, stacked rocks mark a path's entrance. A dirt trail bordering naupaka bushes leads to a rocky shoreline perfect for fishing. A roped off area fronts Paradise Cove, where public entry is forbidden. At most sunsets, Paradise Cove performs the hukilau (Hawaiian fishing ceremony) for the entertainment of its patrons.

Access 73
Ko ʻOlina

In the early 1990s Hawaiʻi developer Herbert Horita cut four lagoons and a marina out of the Ko ʻOlina shoreline for the construction of his resort and residential community. He imported sand to create four artificial beaches, one in each lagoon. There is limited public parking at all of the lagoons. Most of the locals are found at lagoon four as it has the biggest parking lot. Ko ʻOlina Resort has become a popular recreation area not only for visitors worldwide, but for the surrounding communities as well.

A few of the activities at Ko ʻOlina Lagoons are body boarding, snorkeling, and swimming. There is no surfing or fishing allowed inside the lagoons, although experienced surfers and spear divers frequent the outer ocean. Facilities include showers, bathrooms and grassy shores for picnicking. There are bike racks to park your bike. Biking is not allowed on the lagoon walkway, but the roads leading to the lagoons have adequate bike lines, safe speed limits, and slow to moderate traffic. No open fires, umbrellas, or canopies are allowed on the beach. Shade is provided by trees and resort umbrellas on a first-come first-served basis. The lagoon crawl is popular with local athletes who swim/run swim/run all four lagoons then swim/run back.

Access 74
Malakole Camp

This beach access is located in Campbell Industrial Park. To get there, take the Campbell Industrial Park exit off the H1 freeway. Proceed towards the ocean (makai) on Kalaeloa Boulevard. At the second light, turn right on Malakole Street. Pass the Chevron Refinery and turn left on Kaiholo Street. Follow it until it dead-ends. No parking is allowed on the cul-de-sac or street. A parking lot behind the locked gate was closed when we explored the area. We were told cars parked on the street are occasionally towed.

Walking past the gated parking lot you will see a sandy beach leading up to a coral reef. There are tide pools to explore, and ample shore fishing. We saw spinner dolphins playing in the water with two tour boats cruising close to observe them. Boats come out of Ko 'Olina's marina located about .5 miles along the shoreline to the west. Only experienced swimmers and divers go exploring outside this reef's shark infested waters.

The nearest facilities are about .7 miles away at the entrance to Barbers Point Harbor. Retrace your path on Kaiholo Street to Malakole Street and turn left. Follow the road until it dead-ends at the Marisco complex. On the left is a driveway by Phoenician LLC and the shipyard. Turn left and proceed to the parking lot for the private boat harbor. Parking for the general public is left of the boat launch and contains a bathroom, but no shower facilities. If you have four-wheel drive, there is a rocky path that leads over a berm to a sandy shore where people camp, fish, and off-road.

Added Access

Listed by the City and County after 2008, this is a previously undocumented access. This access is full of trash, dirty sand and graffitied construction debris. The odor from nearby manufacturers is most unpleasant. The only activity here is fishing. Parking is available, but there are no other public amenities.

Barber's Point Beach Park
91-021 OLAI STREET

This desolate seven-acre beach park is located at the western tip of Campbell Industrial Park, next to the Barber's Point Lighthouse and Germaine's Lū'au. Take Kalaeloa Boulevard, exit 1 off the H1 freeway until it ends at Olai Street. Turn right on Olai Street and follow to the end of the road. The park is not well maintained with dusty dried up grass and a few picnic tables. The narrow beach is enclosed by a reef shelf with tide pools. Not good for swimming, the area is more conducive to shore fishing. The surf break off shore is for intermediate surfers, but beware of sharks. There are restrooms, showers and parking available but no lifeguards are on duty.

The park takes its name from Captain Henry Barber who wrecked his ship, the *Arthur,* here in 1796. He was in route from Honolulu to Kauaʻi when the boat got stuck on the reef. His crew of twenty-two managed to escape, although six men died. The area was formerly known as Kalaeloa or "long point" but was renamed Barber's Point to commemorate the event. The first lighthouse was built nearby in 1888, then replaced with the current lighthouse in 1933, although it is no longer functioning.

Nimitz Beach
CORAL SEA ROAD

Named for Fleet Admiral Chester W. Nimitz, commander-in-chief of the pacific forces, Nimitz Beach is located in Kalaeloa, which was formerly Barber's Point Naval Air Station. The station was decommissioned in 1999 and the beach areas, although still retained by the navy for R&R, are open to the public. To get there exit H1 at the Kalaeloa, Makakilo, Kapolei exit and turn left on Makakilo Drive heading towards the ocean. Follow this road about two miles to the old guard gate and a four-way stop. Turn left on Roosevelt Avenue and follow approximately one mile, turn right at Coral Sea Road. The road winds past the airfield and continues to parallel the beach. Just past the navy cabins on the left and across from the Coast

Guard station is Nimitz Beach. There are restrooms and shady picnic pavilions. They have recently started locking the gates and closing the beach on weekdays. It is a narrow sandy beach with crystal clear waters. The wave action is minimal most of the year, although a large north swell has been known to wrap around this south facing beach in the winter. Swimming is popular at the west end of the park near the jetty. A popular fishing beach, sea life is also found in tide pools further west past the jetty. "Swabyland" surf spot located just past the reef is named in honor of the young enlisted men who frequented this beach.

White Plains Beach Park

This beach, which gets its name from its access White Plains Road, is also located in Kalaeloa. The directions are the same as to Nimitz Beach but you will be turning left on White Plains Road before the road bends toward the ocean. The beach park is located at the end of White Plains Road. It used to be the officer's beach before the base closed. The navy retained the cabins and recreational facilities but the beach is open daily from sunrise to sunset for the public. It is a popular area with a long sandy beach and rolling waves perfect to learn to surf. The rental concessions are still open along with showers, restrooms, and dining pavilions on a tree-lined grassy stretch fronting the beach. The beach has designated swimming and surfing areas with lifeguards on duty most days. This is an excellent spot to start a biking adventure. Retrace your White Plains Road drive on the bike and head down towards Nimitz Beach. Be sure to stop on the road just across from the airstrip when you get your first ocean view. Monk seals are known to sun themselves on the beach near the Diamond Head end. If you ride towards the mountains from White Plains Beach, pass around the metal gates to a deserted road that eventually borders the Barber's Point Golf Course and 'Ewa Marina Golf Course. The road is blocked off from traffic so it is safe to bring the kids with their bikes. End the adventure at the park with a picnic and a cooling swim.

Kapolei History

A ccess 72 at Paradise Cove has a unique and ancient history. Queen Ka'ahumanu, the favorite wife of King Kamehameha I, bathed and performed sacred rituals in the three natural lagoons west of Ko 'Olina's four man-made ones. In 1939, Alice Kamokila Campbell leased thirty-seven acres of this beachfront property and named it Lanikūhonua or "where heaven meets earth." Hawaiian history refers to accesses 72 and 73 as Ko 'Olina or "Place of Joy" as it was a favorite vacationing spot of High Chief Kakuhihewa. During World War II, the area adjacent to Paradise Cove was used as a recreation center by army and navy. Fishermen know the cove for its delectable thread fish or "moi." It's a perfect location for the aforementioned Paradise Cove Hukilau.

Campbell Industrial Park at access 74 is named for James Campbell, who in the late 1800s purchased 41,000 acres of flat, fruitless, and dry land on O'ahu's Leeward Side. Other Honolulu businessmen called him insane, but Campbell drilled wells to irrigate sugar cane fields for a prolific monetary yield. Kapolei now sits on those sugar cane fields. In 1877 Campbell married Abigail Kuaihel- ani Maipinepine Bright. Their daughter Alice would later create Lanikūhonua. Prior to WWII, Camp Malakole was used as an army camp, housing men in tents. Three men stationed there, Sgt Henry C Blackwell, Cpl Clyde C Brown, and Sgt Warren D Rasmussen unwittingly became the first American casual- ties of Pearl Harbor after they rented two piper cub airplanes from Honolulu Airport to practice their piloting skills. On the morning of December 7,1941 they were shot down after coming upon Japanese Zeros off the 'Ewa coast.

Kalaeloa Community Development District now controls most of the land of what was once Barber's Point Naval Air Station. After part of a nation-wide military base downsizing that took place in 1999, the original Hawaiian name of the point, Kalaeloa, was reapplied.

In 1990 Kapolei consisted of Barber's Point Naval Air Station and a few sur- rounding communities. By 2010 Kapolei's population had skyrocketed, and ground was broken for another O'ahu courthouse there. Plans for shopping malls and University of Hawai'i's West O'ahu campus ensure this second city will become a reality.

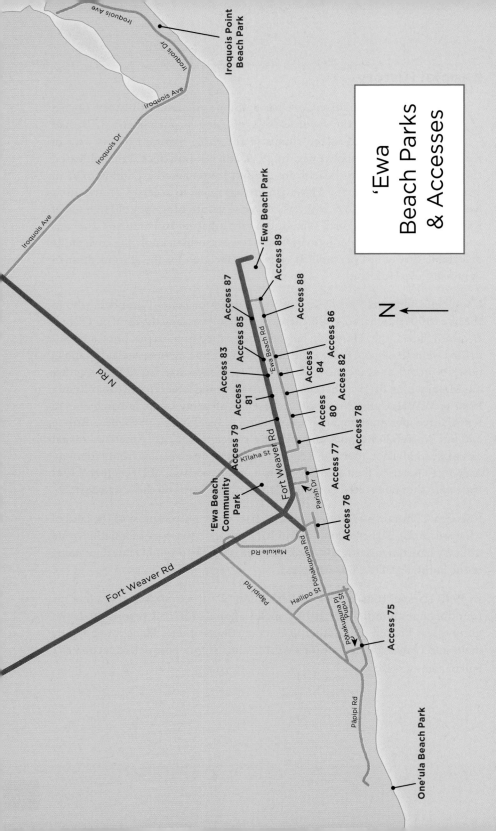

'Ewa
Beach Parks
& Accesses

N

Iroquois Point Beach Park

Iroquois Ave

Iroquois Dr

Iroquois Ave

Iroquois Dr

Iroquois Ave

'Ewa Beach Park

Access 89

Access 88

Access 87

Access 86

Access 85

Ewa Beach Rd

Access 84

Access 83

Access 82

Access 81

Access 80

Access 79

Access 78

Kīlaha St

Access 77

Parish Dr

Access 76

'Ewa Beach Community Park

Fort Weaver Rd

N Rd

Fort Weaver Rd

Makule Rd

Pōhākupuna Rd

Papipi Rd

Hailipo St

Pōhākupuna Pl

Pupu St

Access 75

Papipi Rd

One'ula Beach Park

'EWA
Beach Parks and Accesses 75 to 89

'Ewa Beach shimmers like a pearl with glistening waves rolling in from distant Diamond Head and Waikīkī. The term "'ewa" means "stray" in Hawaiian. Hawaiian legend tells us of two Gods playing a game of rolling stones, and one stone going astray to land in the area that is now 'Ewa. Please be aware that accesses 79, 81, 83, 85, and 87 are byways that connect Fort Weaver Road to Ewa Beach Road where the actual beach access is located. The fifteen accesses to find this hidden treasure are between One'ula Beach Park and 'Ewa Beach Park. All of these 'Ewa Beach accesses have stunning Diamond Head views. Distant Waikīkī skyscrapers and hotels sparkle like diamonds from across the horizon. Shells and coral litter the beach at high tide, along with box jellyfish every ten days after the full moon. Stay clear of those .. they hurt! The neighborhood is a mishmash of older kama'āina homes, upscale cosmopolitan cottages and shanties ready for demolition. Silva's store, Teddy's Barber Shop, and The Church of God in Christ take you back to a time when neighborhoods were small and friendly. Once you access the beach, it's truly old Hawai'i, where small kids scour the reef with nets in tow looking for the ever elusive eel or octopus. At this remote refuge we saw people with their dogs playing in the water.

The 'Ewa accesses are reached by traveling west on H1 from Honolulu and exiting on 5A 'Ewa West, Fort Weaver Road. Continue traveling five miles down Fort Weaver Road past the 'Ewa Beach Shopping Center. See individual access numbers for further instructions. Bus Route 42 from Waikīkī or Honolulu will get you to the 'Ewa Transit Center, then transfer to the 44 bus which will take you to all the accesses. The traffic here is minimal and we saw bikers, including small local children cruising through the rights of way and neighborhood streets. Drivers need to be observant and go slow. Bicycling on Geiger Road to Iroquois Point is for more experienced bikers as there are places where the bike lane narrows or is non-existent. The lanes are better and the traffic minimal inside Iroquois Point.

One'ula Beach Park
91-101 PĀPIPI ROAD

One'ula means "red sand." After heavy rains, large quantities of red sand once emptied onto the beach and into the ocean. The red dirt that mixed with the sand is likely the origin of the name. Just past 'Ewa Beach Shopping Center take a right on Pāpipi Road and drive 1.5 miles to the stop sign. Keep going straight. This park is run-down. Although the thick sandy beaches have good surfing, swimming, snorkeling, and fishing, there is no warm fuzzy feeling from the crowd hanging out. We recommend 'Ewa Beach Park over One'ula Beach Park which is on the other side of this long stretch of beach and next to access 89. Surfers enjoy a number of breaks including "John's," Sand Tracks," and "Chicken Creek." The beach to the east of One'ula Beach Park is called Hau Bush for the groves of hau trees that line the back shore. Formerly a private recreation area for employees of the 'Ewa Sugar Company, Hau Bush is leased and maintained by the Kālia Lions Club International. Surf sites include Hau Bush and Shark Country. The park's restrooms and showers are functional. This beach has been an area of focus over the years due to its reputation as a dumping ground and homeless encampment. The community is actively working on beach clean-ups and closing the park at night to make the area cleaner and safer.

Access 75
END OF PŌHAKUPUNA PLACE
AND PŪPŪ STREET

From the 'Ewa Beach Shopping Center turn right at the first light after the shopping center onto Pāpipi Road. Follow the road .8 miles until you reach Pōhakupuna Road on the left. Turn left, take the first right onto Pōhakupuna Place. It will dead-end at Pūpū Street, where the access is located. Sign 188A marks

the entrance. There is reasonable parking on the street. Too rocky for swimming, snorkeling, or boogie boarding, but exploring tide pools, and reef fishing may be possible at low tide. Better accesses for those activities are eastward. This area is known to locals as Little Seawall. Big Seawall is west on Pūpū Place, but it is not a public access way.

Access 76
ONE'ULA PLACE

To reach this access from 'Ewa Beach Shopping Center continue down Fort Weaver Road to Makule Street, the first right after the light at Pāpipi Road. Continue on Makule Street until it dead-ends on One'ula Place. Turn right and the access is on the left marked 187A.

This secluded sandy beach is perfect for fishing and snorkeling or boogie boarding beyond the reef. The beach is narrow, only fifteen feet at high tide. Looking east during low tide you could probably walk this long stretch of sandy beach which is approachable through the next twelve access ways. To the west the beach ends at a rocky seawall during high tide. Facilities are available at One'ula Beach Park and 'Ewa Beach Park.

Access 77
PARISH DRIVE

To get to this access follow Fort Weaver Road past the 'Ewa Beach Shopping Center down Fort Weaver Road. Right after the road bends to the east you will turn right on Parish Drive. Follow Parish Drive to about the middle of the loop and the access is on your right, marked by sign 186J.

Twenty feet of sandy beach is available at high tide and connects to other accesses via this beach. Fishing and snorkeling are doable. From here to access 89 are gems of topaz skyline, sapphire waters, and sun-basking sand. Access 89 is adjacent 'Ewa Beach Community Park where superior bathrooms and shower facilities are available.

Limu Management Area

A limu management area begins at access 77. No one may pick or harvest the limu without a permit from the beach extending out into the ocean 150 feet, and from Mu'umu'u Street (access 78) to the gunnery range (east of 'Ewa Beach park). Limu is a type of seaweed that is a part of the Hawaiian diet. It is used as a vegetable either eaten with fish and poi or mixed in stews or salads. An excellent source of many vitamins and minerals, over harvesting has resulted in declining availability of this island delicacy.

Access 78
'EWA BEACH ROAD

This access can be reached by traveling down Fort Weaver Road past the 'Ewa Beach Shopping Center at Kīlaha Street. A right turn will get you on 'Ewa Beach Road, the access marked 186 I is directly in front of you as you reach the

"T" in the road. Parking is available on the shoulders of both sides of the street. This begins a one-mile stretch of accesses that connect Fort Weaver Road to 'Ewa Beach Road and 'Ewa Beach Road to the ocean.

The beach is narrow, only about ten feet wide at high tide. The reef extends out another couple of hundred feet. Fishing and squiding are popular activities at low tide when the reef is exposed. One hundred feet to the right of the access is a pocket of sand for swimmers although a trash-laden storm runoff empties into the ocean here, making it favorable for sharks.

Access 79
FORT WEAVER ROAD

The 186G sign marks a pass through from Fort Weaver Road to Ewa Beach Road where access 80 is located. Parking is available on the north side of Fort Weaver Road. Located between the Church of God in Christ Prayer Center on the east and Teddy's Barber Shop on the west, this access is through a hidden and empty lot so use caution.

Access 80
'EWA BEACH ROAD

Marked 186H, this access is located just east of Silva's Grocery and Liquor store. Parking is available across the street in an empty lot. Tide pools are to the west, where at low tide many locals were seen poking in the rocks looking for squid and using nets to catch eels. Most of the homes have seawalls with about twenty feet of sand fronting the reef. The beach narrows to the west. About three hundred feet to the east is a small sandy pocket for swimming, but kayaking and fishing are the preferred activities here.

Access 81
FORT WEAVER ROAD

186G marks another pass-through access from Fort Weaver Road, where you can park on the north side of Fort Weaver Road. This access takes you to access 82 on 'Ewa Beach Road. The path is behind the fire hydrant and between two concrete walls.

Access 82
'EWA BEACH ROAD

Sign 186F marks an entry between a coral rock and wood fence, where there is a narrow beach at low tide. At high tide, the sea washes up against the seawalls fronting the houses.

Access 83
FORT WEAVER ROAD

Sign 186E is located next to a bike route sign and a bus stop. You pass through here to access 84 on 'Ewa Beach Road.

Access 84
'EWA BEACH ROAD

Chain-link fence lines both sides of this access to the beach, marked 186D. About one hundred feet west of the access is a small sandy pocket to play in. A surf spot is located just beyond the reef. Boogie boarding and kayaking were activities spotted here.

Access 85
FORT WEAVER ROAD

Sign 186C marks another access used to pass through to access 86 on 'Ewa Beach Road

Access 86
'EWA BEACH ROAD

A walkway marked 186B is located between a chain-link fence and coral rock wall. A small amount of shade from a palm tree at the end of this walkway provides a cool spot on a hot day. Boogie boarders can play beyond the coral reef. Trees providing shade make this a pleasant spot to spend time. Swimming pockets are to the east.

Access 87
FORT WEAVER ROAD

Sign 186A marks a pass-through to access 88 on 'Ewa Beach Road.

Access 88
‘EWA BEACH ROAD

185C marks a dirt driveway going straight to the beach, where some nice shade from an ironwood tree is located to the east.

Access 89
‘EWA BEACH ROAD

185A marks a sign that is easily missed because it is behind a tree to the left of the arrow sign. Take the path between the block wall and the chain-link fence to the beach. This shallow reef is perfect for shore casting and kayaking. If you want to swim, walk eastward about three hundred feet to ‘Ewa Beach Park, where there is a reef break.

‘Ewa Beach Park
91-027 FORT WEAVER ROAD

Located at the end of Fort Weaver Road, directly across from the ‘Ewa Beach Golf Club, ‘Ewa Beach Park has stunning views towards Diamond Head and the city skyline. The park provides many activities, along with a pavilion, bathrooms, showers, playground, baseball diamond, basketball courts, and a parking lot large enough to accommodate many vehicles. The park is frequented by locals on the weekends and nearly deserted on weekdays. The wide white sandy beach provides great sunbathing and the reef break accommodates swimming, kayaking, shore casting, and outrigger canoeing. There is a surf break off shore that can be crowded if conditions are good. If you choose to swim, beware as there are dangerous currents and no lifeguards.

Iroquois Point Beach Park

To get to this secluded beach take Fort Weaver Road, then turn left at Geiger Road and follow the road as it skirts the edges of the former military facility. Turn right at the sign for Waterfront at Puʻuloa. A guard gate is located about .25 miles down this road where you must obtain a visitor pass before entry is allowed. This beach community was formerly Iroquois Point Naval Magazine but was turned over to private developers in 2003 in an exchange for infra-structure and other construction improvements on Ford Island. Restricting public access to the beach was an issue back then, but it was resolved by 2008 when the area opened to the public. With Diamond Head as the backdrop, the beach offers excellent views of the entrance to Pearl Harbor and planes taking off from the reef runway of Honolulu Airport. Fishing, kayaking, swimming, and surfing are some of the enjoyable activities here. The beach is open from sunrise to sunset with twenty-three public parking stalls. Restrooms and showers are available, but no lifeguards are on duty. The chairs and cabanas lining the beach are reserved for residents of the area.

ʻEwa History

This beachside community was originally called Kūpaka, the Hawaiian name for tobacco. Renamed ʻEwa Beach by postmaster Harry K. Ching in the 1930s, Ching found the original name of Kūpaka too difficult for foreign newcomers to pronounce, much less remember. ʻEwa town, a few miles away, contained the former sugar mill which in those days employed many in this beachside community. As a prime sugar producer, ʻEwa made use of its lusciously fertile soil and vegetation. A decade later the sugar production in this profitable town dissolved, but ʻEwa Beach remade herself into a self sustained village, frequented by both local and foreign adventurers. ʻEwa Beach has a bevy of golf courses: ʻEwa Villages, Coral Creek, and Hawaiʻi Prince are a few of them. Sports enthusiasts might find the name of the place familiar as the ʻEwa Beach team beat the team from Curacao to win 2005's Little League World Series.

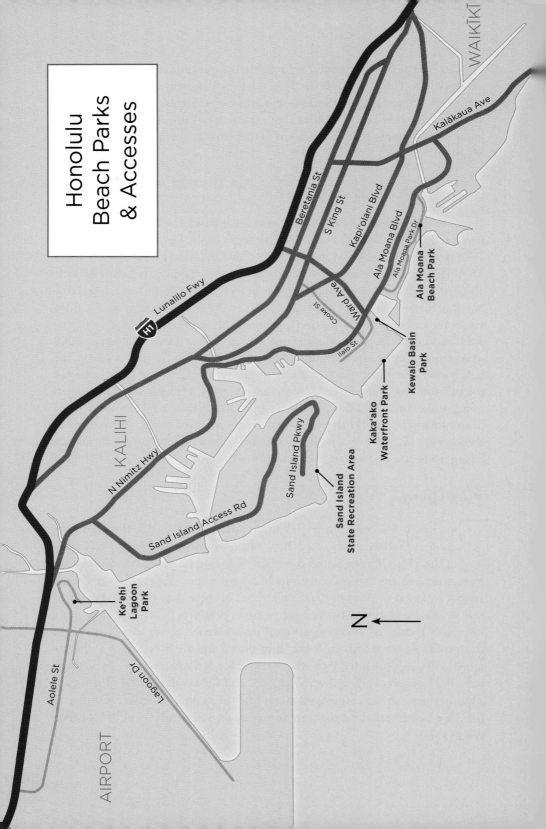

Honolulu
Beach Parks
& Accesses

WAIKĪKĪ

Kalākaua Ave

Beretania St

S King St

Kapi'olani Blvd

Ala Moana Blvd

Ala Moana Park Dr

Ala Moana
Beach Park

Ward Ave

Cooke St

Ilalo St

Kewalo Basin
Park

Kaka'ako
Waterfront Park

Lunalilo Fwy

H1

N Nimitz Hwy

KALIHI

Sand Island Pkwy

Sand Island
State Recreation Area

Sand Island Access Rd

Ke'ehi
Lagoon Park

N

Aolele St

Lagoon Dr

AIRPORT

HONOLULU
Beach Parks

T hroughout the urban jungle of Honolulu are hidden pockets of refuge where reclaimed land has been transformed into retreats for the soul. Honolulu meaning "protected harbor" is host to five beach parks that provide unique vantage points of the sunny southern shore, Diamond Head and breathtaking sunsets backed by towering city skyscrapers. Conveniently located in the center of town, picking up a picnic lunch or pūpūs and heading to these beach parks allows weary workers a brief respite from their busy lives. This section covers the urban beach parks located on the South Shore from Keʻehi Lagoon to Ala Moana Beach Park.

Keʻehi Lagoon Park
465 LAGOON DRIVE

This seventy-two-acre park is located in Honolulu just minutes from the Honolulu Airport. To get there from Waikīkī take Ala Wai Boulevard to Niu Street and turn left. Continue on Ala Moana Boulevard; it becomes Nimitz Highway. Just after passing Sand Island Access Road move to the left lane and proceed on Nimitz Highway under the highway. Turn left on Lagoon Drive, take another left at the third light on Aolele Street. The tennis courts are on your right as you enter the park. The area is widely used by canoe clubs and boaters with some areas used for fishing. There is very little beach to speak of so other ocean activities are not recommended. The park offers plenty of grassy ball fields for baseball and soccer along with a pavilion, restrooms, and tennis courts. Barbecues and picnic tables are sprinkled throughout the park. This is a nice starting point for a bike ride along Lagoon Drive. The panoramic view is awe inspiring from the verdant Koʻolau mountains to the sky scrapers on the Honolulu waterfront, and aquamarine ocean beyond. The road terminates at the end of the reef runway of Honolulu Airport which provides an excellent perspective for watching departing and landing planes of all sizes. Cyclists routinely use Lagoon Drive for training due to the flat grade and light traffic in the area.

Just off shore is tiny ten-acre Mokauea Island, the site of one of the last surviving pre-European coastal Hawaiian fishing villages. The island with its unique historical and cultural value was nearly destroyed in the 1940s when the Kalihi Channel was dredged for western access to Honolulu Harbor. Later in the 1970s, the state got into a dispute with the families that had lived there for generations, accusing them of squatting on state property. They burned down some of the houses but stopped after public outcry. They negotiated an agreement for a sixty-five-year lease with the families and stipulated a learning center be built on the island to provide scientific study opportunities and help restore the village to its traditional Hawaiian practices.

Sand Island State Recreation Area
END OF SAND ISLAND ACCESS ROAD

This urban Honolulu beach park is located at the end of Sand Island Access Road at the entrance to Honolulu Harbor. To get there take Nimitz Highway, turn left towards the ocean at Sand Island Access Road, continue over the bridge until the road dead-ends at the park. Take the 19 Bus that stops at Nimitz Highway and Pu'uhale Road; it's just over a mile walk to the park entrance.

This man-made island was formed by filling in the reef with detritus from dredging Honolulu Harbor and Ke'ehi Lagoon. The unique location of this park affords views of Diamond Head, the Honolulu waterfront and various planes overhead taking off from Honolulu International Airport. You will find the remnants of military use such as deserted lookout towers and bunkers from World War II. The area was used by the military during World War II for defending the coast and downtown. It is also the site of the largest internment camp on O'ahu for Japanese Americans rounded up during the period of martial law after the attack at Pearl Harbor.

Activities are limited to fishing, surfing and swimming, but stay near shore since this area has heavy boat traffic. The surf break is located right off the sandy beach area and aligns with the watch tower. There is plenty of parking with restrooms, picnic tables, covered pavilions, BBQ grills, and weekend camping. Permits are available from the Department of Land and Natural Resources (see useful websites for more information). There are no lifeguards on duty so swim at your own risk. The gates close at 6:45 PM in the fall and winter (from the weekend after Labor Day until March 31) and 7:45 PM in the spring and summer (April 1 until the Friday after Labor Day). The gates do not reopen until 7 AM the next morning; cars cannot enter or leave during that period.

Kaka'ako Waterfront Park
677 ALA MOANA BOULEVARD

To reach this park follow Ala Moana Boulevard west, pass Ward Avenue. and turn left on 'Ohe Street towards the ocean. Follow 'Ohe Street until it dead-ends into the parking area. By bus take the 19 Bus westbound and exit at Ward Avenue. Cross Ala Moana Boulevard and walk towards the ocean; Ward Avenue. becomes Ilalo Street. Turn left at the third street which is Ohe Street and continue towards the ocean until you reach the park.

This former landfill has been turned into a delightful metropolitan park complete with grassy rolling hills, covered pavilions with picnic tables, and views that are unparalleled. It is an awe-inspiring location to catch views of sunsets and surfers. The park is sandwiched between Honolulu Harbor and Kewalo Basin. The west tip of the park ends at Pier 1 of Honolulu Harbor making it an excellent spot to watch barge traffic traveling in and out of the harbor. At the east end of the park is Kewalo Basin boat channel where commercial fishing and tour boats can be seen entering and exiting the harbor. Just across the boat channel is Kewalo Basin Park which connects to Ala Moana Beach Park. There is no beach here but the area is heavily used by fishermen, surfers, and body boarders. The area to the east is well known to boogie boarders as "Point Panic," a prime spot that does not allow board surfing. Surf sites include "Incinerators" and "Flies," no doubt a reference to the trash incinerator and landfill that was located nearby years ago. There are areas to swim directly in front of the park with stairs leading down to the ocean. Stay clear of the west end due to the heavy barge traffic. Cardboard sliding on the grassy hills as well as biking or skating on the paved trails are favorite family activities here. There is an amphitheater at the park which has been a popular outdoor venue for various concerts. A monument located here is a tribute to the nine Japanese sailors who lost their lives in 2001 on the *Ehime Maru* educational fishing vessel. The U.S. nuclear submarine *Greeneville* accidently struck their boat and it sank within five minutes.

Kewalo Basin Park
1075 ALA MOANA BOULEVARD

To reach this little known park take Ala Moana Boulevard west, at Ward Avenue make a U-turn and take an immediate right on the access road, drive to the east around the boat harbor. At the end of the road there is a free parking lot that allows access to the park. The basin was dredged in 1925 to ease the traffic at Honolulu Harbor for small commercial fishing boats. The harbor still hosts commercial fishing and tour boats with most of the tour boat activities originating here. At the ocean's edge, the park was developed on a section of former landfill. The area is widely used by fishermen, surfers, swimmers, stand up paddle boarders, and picnickers. There are a couple of surf sites located off shore, "Kewalos" being the most well known. Kewalos is located at the west end of the park nearest to the boat channel. Fishing and reef walking are excellent activities here because there is wading access towards Ala Moana Reef without having to swim out to it. The small park has a scenic brick promenade fronting the ocean next to the seawall, making it an excellent viewing spot from Diamond Head to 'Ewa. There are shaded pavilions, picnic tables and an 8,400 square foot net shed for fishermen. Restrooms and showers are also available.

Ala Moana Beach Park
1201 ALA MOANA BOULEVARD

Conveniently located right in the center of town across from Ala Moana Shopping Center, Ala Moana Beach Park and Magic Island are two of the more well known beach spots on the island. Ala Moana which means "Path to the Sea" and Magic Island also known as 'Āina Moana, which means "Land from the Sea" comprise the two sections of the park. This park is very family friendly with about one hundred acres of manicured lawns, a plethora of shade trees, and a golden sandy beach. The beach is flat, the water is shallow and generally devoid of waves most of the year which makes it a favorite spot for swimmers and small children. There is another beach lagoon located at the tip of Magic Island that provides sheltered swimming too. The reef area about fifty yards out has sharp coral and jagged rocks so care should be taken if swimming out there. Only experienced swimmers should go beyond the reef due to strong undercurrents and the presence of paddle boarders and surfers. Some surf spots located just off shore from east to west are "Ala Moana Bowls," "Big Lefts Big Rights," "Bomboras," "Concessions," "Courts," and "Point Panic" at the edge of Kewalo Basin. Avoid swimming or surfing in front of the boat channels bordering both sides of the park. This park is also a favorite of joggers and bikers who can enjoy oceanside paved trails.

Lifeguards staff the beach year round. There are food concessions in the park along with picnic tables, restrooms, showers, phones, tennis courts, and plenty of grass for croquet or lawn bowling.

Honolulu History

The South Shore of Oʻahu was once swampland with fishponds built by ancient Hawaiians, but through the years industry has molded the shoreline to fit its purpose. Along with harbors, dumps, and landfills, a number of shoreline parks were developed. In the early 1900s Hawaiian Dredging bought land in an area known as Kālia to dump earth and coral from their many dredging projects. A channel was dredged nearby in the 1920s to connect Ala Wai Boat Harbor with Kewalo Basin. Eventually the swampland was filled in and the area became more popular. In the 1950s, the west end of the channel was closed to accommodate a landfill at Kewalo Basin and sand was shipped in to form the beach. The parcel of land was dedicated in 1934 by President Roosevelt as Moana Park, the name was changed to Ala Moana Beach Park in 1947. The following year Walter Dillinghams's son, Lowell, built the icon Ala Moana Shopping Center directly across the street from the park. In the early 1960s another landfill project produced Magic Island; originally planned as a resort area, it never came to fruition. The land was transferred to the state and dedicated in the early 1970s as ʻĀina Moana Park.

Kewalo Basin, one of the three commercial harbors on Oʻahu, was originally built to accommodate lumber schooners in the 1920s. Unfortunately that trade began to dry up before the harbor was completed. Commercial fisherman took up residence and still exist there today alongside tour boats offering scuba diving, parasailing, catamaran rides and dinner cruises. University of Hawaiʻi maintains a marine research facility, Kewalo Basin Laboratory, where they study biodiversity and the effects of human activity on the marine environment. The access to coral reef ecosystems provides opportunities to train university students, and perform outreach activities.

The area around Sand Island became important in the early 1800s when Kamehameha moved his court to Kou, a village just north of there. As Honolulu Harbor grew in size so did Sand Island due to its safe and convenient berthing for large ships and a wealth of ocean resources. Sand Island began as a coral reef with natural stream channels on the east and west ends of the island. The channel and the harbor were dredged numerous times to support more ocean-going vessels and the detritus was dumped on the reef, eventually forming the island. In the 1860s, Kamehameha III's government used one of the smaller islands as a quarantine area for ship passengers who had contracted smallpox. It became known as Quarantine Island and in 1916 was turned into the Sand Island Military Reservation. It served duty as the headquarters for the Army Port and Service Command as well as the largest internment camp on the island for Japanese Americans during World War II. In 1959, the military turned the land over to the Territory of Hawaiʻi, which became the State of Hawaiʻi that year. The park's reputation has suffered from neglect and abuse by the homeless population over the last twenty years, but has been cleaned out recently. The state entered an agreement with a non-profit to establish an off roading area named the Sandbox in an undeveloped section of the park. It provides sorely needed acceptable off-roading tracks for BMX, four-wheel drive, and motocross activities.

Dredging and filling in the 1940s to accommodate boat moorings altered Keʻehi Lagoon, originally a shallow reef. In the 1970s construction of Honolulu Airport's reef runway further changed the lagoon along with the dredging of three seaplane runways. No beach was ever made in the area, but the boating community enjoys use of the area with small sailboats and canoe regattas dominating in the summer months.

Bibliography

Clark, John R. K. *Beaches of O'ahu*. Revised edition. Honolulu: University of Hawai'i Press, 2005.

———. *Hawai'i Place Names: Shores, Beaches, and Surf Sites*. Honolulu: University of Hawai'i Press, 2005.

Dorrance, William H. *O'ahu's Hidden History*. Honolulu: Mutual Publishing, 1999.

Doughty, Andrew. *O'ahu Revealed: The Ultimate Guide to Honolulu, Waikiki & Beyond*. 2nd Edition. Lihue, HI: Wizard Publications, Inc., 2007.

DrBeach.org. "The Best Beach in America." http://www.drbeach.org/top10beaches.htm (accessed August 8, 2008).

Foster, Jeanette. *Frommer's Honolulu, Waikiki & Oahu*. 10th Edition. Hoboken, NJ: Wiley Publishing, Inc. 2008.

Gomes, Andrew. "Hawaii Kai home sells for $15.9 million." *Honolulu Advertiser,* November 9, 2007. http://the.honoluluadvertiser.com/article/2007/Nov/09/bz/hawaii711090355.html.

Harold K. L. Castle Foundation. *About Us*. May 3, 2008. http://www.castlefoundation.org/founder-history.htm.

Hawaii Aviation Preservation Society. "Haleiwa Field." http://hiavps.com/haleiwa.htm (accessed December 5, 2009).

Hawaii Reserves, Inc. "Envision Laie." http://www.hawaiireserves.com/pdf/Envision_Laie_newsletter.pdf.

———. "News and Events." http://www.hawaiireserves.com/ (accessed August 3, 2008).

Hawaii State Info. "Kaneohe, Honolulu County, Hawaii." http://www.hawaiistateinfo.com/kaneohe.php (accessed August 4, 2008).

HawaiiWeb.com "Oahu Activities." http://www.hawaiiweb.com/oahu/beaches/default.htm (accessed August 3, 2008).

Historic Fort Barrette-Puu O Kapolei. "Camp Malakole – December 7, 1941 – Three 251st AA Soldiers Killed By Japanese Planes." http://www.december7.com/1941/Fort_Barrette/page5.html.

Honolulu International Airport. "Dillingham Air Field (HDH)." http://hawaii.gov/hnl/airport-information/dillingham-air-field (accessed July 5, 2008).

James, Van. *Ancient Sites of O'ahu*. Revised edition. Honolulu: Bishop Museum Press, 2010.

Kaneohe Ranch Management Ltd. "Overview History." http://www.kaneoheranch.com/history (accessed August 4, 2008).

Leone, Dianne. "Dangerous Ground at Sandy Beach." *Star-Bulletin,* March 24, 2002. http://archives.starbulletin.com/2002/03/24/news/story3.html.

Mālama 'Āina Foundation. "History of Ko'olaupoko." http://www.malamaaina.org/files/hawaiian_culture/koolaupoko.pdf (accessed August 5, 2008).

North Shore Chamber of Commerce. "History of the North Shore Chamber of Commerce." http://www.gonorthshore.org/history.htm (accessed December 5, 2009).

O'ahu Beach Directory. "O'ahu's Guarded Beaches." http://www.aloha.com/~lifeguards/bech_dir.html.

Park, Gene. "Iroquois Point beach to open to public." *Star-Bulletin*, March 20, 2008. http://archives.starbulletin.com/2008/03/20/news/story09.html.

Perez, Rob. "Deadline approaches for Kaiser estate bidding." *Star-Bulletin*, February 13, 1997. http://archives.starbulletin.com/97/02/13/business/story5.html.

Piehl, Galen. "Oahu Snorkeling Hawaii Guide." http://www.tropicalsnorkeling.com/oahu-snorkeling-hawaii.html (accessed August 3, 2008).

Roig, Suzanne. "Increase in drownings spurs push to educate." *Honolulu Advertiser*, June 18, 2006. http://the.honoluluadvertiser.com/article/2006/Jun/18/ln/FP606180362.html.

Sanburn, Curt. *A Pocket Guide to O'ahu*. Honolulu: Mutual Publishing 2000.

Sanburn, Curt, Steven Goldsberry, U'i Goldsberry, Glen Grant, Waimea Williams, and Carrie Ching. *A Pocket Guide to Diamond Head and Waikīkī*. Honolulu: Mutual Publishing, 2002.

Shapiro, Treena. "From Rice Fields to High Finance." *Star-Bulletin*, October 8, 1999. http://archives.starbulletin.com/1999/10/08/news/story9.html.

The Southern California Scenic Railway Association, Inc. "A Typical Narrow Gauge Story: the Oahu Railway." http://www.scsra.org/library/oahurwy.html (accessed January 27, 2008).

Sullivan, Richard. *Driving & Discovering Hawai'i: O'ahu*. Los Angeles: Montgomery Ewing Publishers, 2001.

Thomas, Craig, and Susan Scott. *All Stings Considered: First Aid and Medical Treatment of Hawai'i's Marine Injuries*. Honolulu: University of Hawai'i Press, 1997.

Tsai, Michael. "Oahu Railway and Land Co." *Honolulu Advertiser*, July 2, 2006. http://the.honoluluadvertiser.com/150/sesq2oahurailway.

US Lighthouses. "Barber's Point Lighthouse." http://www.us-lighthouses.com/displaypage.php?LightID=56 (accessed November 30, 2008).

Wageman, Virginia. *Essential Guide to Oahu: Including Waikiki and Honolulu*. Waipahu: Island Heritage, 2002.

Wai'anae Baptist Church. "Boki-Chief of Wai'anae" http://waianaebaptist.org/Waianae%20History%20Items/In%20the%20Beginning.htm.

Index of Beach Parks and Accesses

Kakaʻako Waterfront Park—8, 151
Kalaeōʻio Beach Park—5, 77
Kalama Beach Park—4, 59, 63
Kalanianaʻole Highway/West Halemaʻumaʻu
  Street—3, 38
Kaluanui Beach—5, 79
Kaluanui—5, 80
Kamehameha Highway—5-6, 69-73, 75, 77-
  86, 89, 91, 93-94, 96-103, 107
Kāneʻohe Bay Drive—5, 69
Kāneʻohe Beach Park—5, 70
Kapiʻolani Park—3, 23
Kaupō Beach Park—4, 50
Kawaikuʻi Beach Park—3, 38
Kawailoa Beach Park—6, 101
Kawela Bay—6, 89-90
Kē Iki Road—6, 98
Kē Nui Road—6, 89, 94-96
Keaʻau Beach Park—7, 126
Keʻehi Lagoon Beach Park—8, 149
Kewalo Basin Park—8, 152, 154
Ko ʻOlina—8, 117, 131-134, 137
Kōkeʻe Beach Park—3, 42
Koko Kai Beach Park—4, 42

Kokololio Beach Park—5, 82-83
Kualoa Beach Park—5, 75
Kūhiō Beach Park—3, 22-23
Kuilei Cliffs Beach Park—3, 27
Kuliouʻou Beach Park—3, 40

L

Laenani Neighborhood Beach Park—5, 72
Lāʻie Beach Park—5, 82-84
Lāʻie Point State Wayside—6, 85
Laniākea Beach—6, 102
Laumilo Street/ʻAlaʻihi Street—4, 54
Laumilo Street/ʻEhukai Street—4, 55
Laumilo Street/Hīhīmanu Street—4, 55
Laumilo Street/Hīnālea Street—4, 55
Laumilo Street/Hilu Street—4, 54
Laumilo Street/Kaʻulu Street—4, 55
Laumilo Street/Mānana Street—4, 54
Laumilo Street/Puʻuone Street—4, 54
Laumilo Street/Wailea Street—4, 53
Lēʻahi Beach Park—3, 25-26
Leftovers Beach Access Park—6, 101
Lualualei Beach Park—7, 120
Lumahaʻi Street—4, 43

M

Māʻili Beach Park—7, 119
Mākaha Beach Park—7, 117, 123-125
Makaleha Beach Park—7, 111
Mākālei Beach Park—3, 25
Mākao Beach—5, 81
Makapuʻu Beach Park—4, 50
Mālaekahana State Recreation Area—6, 86
Malakole Camp—8, 133, 137
Mauna Lahilahi Beach Park—7, 117, 122
Maunalua Bay Beach Park—3, 40-41
Milokai Place—5, 66
Mokuʻauia Beach—6, 87
Mokulēʻia Beach Park—7, 113
Mokulua Drive—4, 60-61
Mokulua Drive/Kaiolena Drive—4, 61
Mokulua Drive/Lanipō Drive—4, 60
Moua Street—7, 122

About the Authors

Katherine Garner and Carol Kettner have forty-six years of combined experience enjoying Oʻahu's shores. These beach-loving mothers of surfers have had ample opportunities to fully explore the island's recreation areas. Avid sportswomen, Katherine and Carol have been actively involved in local triathlons, hiking, biking, and a variety of ocean activities.

Katherine, a graduate of Virginia Tech with a BS in Geology, has written numerous online articles on heath and wellness, as well as travel. She currently writes as YogaKat on HubPages.com.

Carol, a graduate of the University of Hawaiʻi at West Oʻahu with a BA in Business Management has written plays through her business, Blue Moon Mystery, a party planning service for social get-togethers.